ASHE Higher Education Report: Volume 33, Number 6
Kelly Ward, Lisa E. Wolf-Wendel, Series Editors

Parental Involvement in Higher Education: Understanding the Relationship Among Students, Parents, and the Institution

Katherine Lynk Wartman
Marjorie Savage

Parental Involvement in Higher Education: Understanding the Relationship Among Students, Parents, and the Institution
Katherine Lynk Wartman and Marjorie Savage
ASHE Higher Education Report: Volume 33, Number 6
Kelly Ward, Lisa E. Wolf-Wendel, Series Editors

ISSN 1551-6970   electronic ISSN 1554-6306   ISBN 978-0-4703-8529-6

The **ASHE Higher Education Report** is part of the Jossey-Bass Higher and Adult Education Series and is published six times a year by Wiley Subscription Services, Inc., A Wiley Company, at Jossey-Bass, 989 Market Street, San Francisco, California 94103-1741.

For subscription information, see the Back Issue/Subscription Order Form in the back of this volume.

CALL FOR PROPOSALS: Prospective authors are strongly encouraged to contact Kelly Ward (kaward@wsu.edu) or Lisa Wolf-Wendel (lwolf@ku.edu). See "About the ASHE Higher Education Report Series" in the back of this volume.

Visit the Jossey-Bass Web site at **www.josseybass.com.**

Printed in the United States of America on acid-free recycled paper.

The **ASHE Higher Education Report** is indexed in CIJE: Current Index to Journals in Education (ERIC), Current Abstracts (EBSCO), Education Index/Abstracts (H.W. Wilson), ERIC Database (Education Resources Information Center), Higher Education Abstracts (Claremont Graduate University), IBR & IBZ: International Bibliographies of Periodical Literature (K.G. Saur), and Resources in Education (ERIC).

Advisory Board

The ASHE Higher Education Report Series is sponsored by the Association for the Study of Higher Education (ASHE), which provides an editorial advisory board of ASHE members.

R5/08

Contents

Executive Summary

Parents of college students have become an enigma to higher education. College and university administrators, staff, and faculty are mystified when they read the media reports of parents' contacting the institution about their students' problems, when they see students call home during an advising appointment, or when parents contact a professor about a grade or assignment. This new level of family involvement does not fit with the personal history of today's educators, nor does it fit with the student development theory they were taught. It also represents a shift in the relationship between student and institution.

Administrators are seeking an explanation about the cultural shift in parent-student relationships they are witnessing. In this monograph, the authors encourage higher education researchers and practitioners to take their own college experience out of the equation as they consider student-family relationships today. They offer alternatives to generational theory, specifically to the work of Neil Howe and William Strauss, in understanding the contemporary phenomenon of parent involvement. Yes, generation does play a role in how today's students view their parents, but so do the high cost of college, the use of technology, changes in how children are parented (particularly those in the middle and upper-middle classes), and demographic shifts in terms of the number of students whose parents also attended college.

How Are Student Affairs Professionals Taught to Think About Students' Relationship with Their Parents?

One of the primary reasons that student affairs administrators struggle to understand parents' involvement is that it is inconsistent with how they understand the parent–college student relationship. Most student development courses emphasize the theory of separation-individuation (particularly that of Chickering) and the idea that acquiring autonomy and independence from parents is a necessary component of emotional adjustment to college. This publication advocates consideration of attachment theory, originally conceived to discuss infants' relationship with their parental caregivers and more recently applied to college students by human development researchers, as an alternative theory to separation-individuation that may help administrators better understand the students and parents they are working with today. According to this theory, secure attachment relationships offer support in times of stress, allowing students to more confidently explore their new environment. Therefore, rather than needing a defined separation or break from parents, students may actually benefit from regular parental contact and support instead (Kenny, 1987). Under this theory, students' calling home just to "check in" is seen as a normal, healthy behavior (Sorokou and Weissbrod, 2005). Attachment theory may offer a clearer lens through which to understand the development of female college students in particular.

The authors recommend that administrators view attachment theory as an alternative or complement to separation-individuation. Faculty in student affairs graduate programs also are encouraged to include the new model in the curriculum for their graduate students and examine how it may inform the traditional theory of separation-individuation. If administrators, current student affairs practitioners, and new professionals to the field understand the value of parental involvement and the positive outcomes this relationship can have on students' growth, perhaps it would quell their fears about students' lack of individuation.

Another problematic theoretical base in the understanding of college students today is the binary differentiation of child and adult. In some contexts both the institution and society view the college student as a child (or adolescent); in others he or she is viewed as an adult. Perhaps we should adopt a new way of regarding college students and their developmental stage that is more flexible (Arnett, 2000a, 2006).

What Are Institutions Doing in Response to Parental Involvement?

In response to the shifting relationship between parents and students and therefore parents and the institution, colleges and universities have implemented a number of services to meet the needs of parents. Applying both high-tech and high-touch techniques to work with this new secondary audience, colleges and universities find parents to be enthusiastic and effective partners in supporting student retention and success; tackling the troubling areas of student life such as campus drinking, safety, and physical and mental health issues; and even providing new funds as donors to special projects and scholarships.

A few institutions have taken the step of spelling out criteria for desired parent outcomes to help parents understand the college experience, support their student's academic and personal growth, and be involved appropriately with their student and with the institution. Just as colleges and universities are creating student learning outcomes as a way to define competencies and skills to be mastered during the college years, parent outcomes can do the same for family members.

This publication suggests an institutional commitment to defining and supporting appropriate parent involvement rather than reacting to the expectations or demands parents might bring to the table.

Are All Parents the Same?

Parent programs that have been up and running for several years have developed methods to meet the needs of the majority of their parents, and they are now beginning to consider the needs of underserved populations. In most cases parent services contribute to increased parental understanding and support of the somewhat privileged majority student population—white, residential, traditional-age students whose parents have been involved throughout their lives, most of whose parents have a college degree. But what about the students who do not fit this profile?

Putting parents and students into their own broad categories (such as "helicopters" and "Millennials") is problematic. In examining the literature closely, we see that the relationships between parents and students, and between parents and the college or university are different based on individual students' characteristics such as gender, cultural background, parents' income, and parents' level of education. We know that in the context of K–12 education, parental involvement is inextricably linked with socioeconomic status (Lareau, 1987). The level of emotional support that parents provide for higher education is also correlated with this variable. The ways that students from lower and higher socioeconomic groups approach the college admissions process differs widely, primarily related to cultural capital, which in turn, sets the stage for how they will approach their relationship with the college or university once they matriculate.

What does this situation mean for future parental relations, the parent-student relationship, and the parent-institution relationship? When serving parents, administrators need to make sure that the middle-class and upper-middle-class standard of behavior does not dictate institutional policy regarding the school's definition of family-school relationships, as it has in K–12 education (Lareau, 1987). Even though some parents have the ability to donate resources to the institution above and beyond tuition dollars, services for parents need to be targeted at and accessible to all parents, regardless of their income or education level.

Foreword

The topic of parental involvement is clearly on the mind of those in higher education. In the past year alone several articles on the topic have appeared in *The Chronicle of Higher Education,* and numerous professional development workshops and audio conferences discussed effectively working with parents of students. Parents and their quest to be involved in their children's college experience have captured the attention of practitioners and researchers in colleges and universities.

Practitioners find themselves dealing with increased calls from parents asking questions: How is my child doing in school? Why did my son get a "C" in the class? Can my daughter get a new roommate? Such questions tend to be viewed negatively as parents meddling in student affairs, and some are concerned that parents' overinvolvement will stifle students' development. But like most issues, this one also has upsides: parents want to help with fundraising, and parents can alert campus practitioners about their students' health issues or other matters that would otherwise have been unknown. The challenge is finding a balance in working with parents, but practitioners can find themselves at a loss as to the best course of action—on the one hand not wanting to alienate parents but on the other wanting to find a way to alleviate parents' concerns in ways that are legal and in the best interests of student development.

Student affairs professionals and faculty facing increased calls from parents can find themselves stymied about why parents are more involved. Is it the cell phone connection that gives parents too much information? Is it just the next stage of life? Whose parents are involved and what types of questions are they asking? Researchers have started to address some of these questions and are likely to continue to do so as the phenomenon of parental involvement continues to evolve.

Katherine Lynk Wartman and Marjorie Savage have entered the conversation about parental involvement in this monograph, *Parental Involvement in Higher Education: Understanding the Relationship Among Students, Parents, and the Institution*. The authors do an outstanding job of not only addressing some of the practical issues of dealing with parents but also, and more important, filling in many of the questions about parental involvement that have gone unanswered. Why are parents more involved? Are particular kinds of parents more likely to be involved? Is parental involvement a good thing for students? Are certain kinds of programs available for parents? Where can I get help to know how best to address particular situations with parents? Wartman and Savage address many of these questions. The authors, who both have firsthand experience in parental involvement programs, fill in and address gaps in understanding about parental involvement in higher education analytically, thoughtfully, thoroughly, and comprehensively.

The monograph provides an overview of parental involvement that starts with addressing the reasons for parental involvement: demographics, technology and theoretical considerations that emerge from the examination of parent-child attachment and student development. This background alone provides a fresh and informed prospective on parental involvement. The authors also grapple with a perennial issue for student affairs practitioners: how best to deal with students as adults. Young adulthood, the stage of the majority of students in four-year colleges, is a transitional one that occupies a limited space between childhood and adulthood. The authors also address some of the nuances associated with parental involvement by discussing topics such as socioeconomic class, race, and gender to provide a fuller understanding of whose parents are likely to be involved and the cultural considerations of parental involvement. In addition, the authors use this information to address what implications involvement has for theory and practice in higher education.

The monograph is also a great resource. The authors provide practical and straightforward recommendations for working with parents from a programmatic and personal standpoint. The monograph also provides valuable information about resources for campuses and practitioners who want to develop or update programs for parents or just to have ideas about how best to address parents' concerns. The recommendations and resources list places to go for information about creating positive relationships with parents that are in the best interest of parents, students, faculty, and staff.

For practitioners and faculty members who want to deal with parents in constructive and positive ways, this monograph is a must read. It provides the requisite background knowledge needed to enhance relationships with parents of students in ways that are proactive and informed. Too often when the call comes from an angry parent, it is not always clear how faculty and practitioners should respond effectively. The information and analysis in this monograph are sure to provide the background information necessary to think holistically about parents and their involvement in their college student's experience.

Kelly Ward
Series Editor

Acknowledgments

This publication is the outcome of a collaborative project begun at an Administrators Promoting Parent Involvement (APPI) conference several years ago. We would like to acknowledge the spirit of support we found among participants at that conference and in our continuing contacts with parent program directors and staff as we developed this manuscript.

In addition, we each had our own guides in the development of our interest in this topic.

From Katherine Lynk Wartman: I would like to acknowledge Ana Martínez Alemán, my advisor in the Higher Education Program at Boston College, who encouraged me to rectify the need I saw for a publication on this topic by writing one myself, as well as Karen Arnold, my other incredible mentor at B.C. I would also like to thank Kelly Ward, editor of the ASHE Higher Education Report series, not only for believing that a doctoral student in the early stages of her career could write a publication such as this but also for being excited about it. In addition, I wish to recognize Anne Ponder, chancellor of the University of North Carolina at Asheville and former president of Colby-Sawyer College who, six years ago, alerted me to the cultural shift in the college-student-parent relationship and then asked me whether I wanted to help the institution understand and manage it by coming to work for her. Finally, I thank my own parents for their many gifts but above all the right balance between support and independence.

From Marjorie Savage: I thank the administrators at the University of Minnesota who have supported the development of parent services and who have encouraged ongoing research on the topic of parent-university relations.

They include my previous supervisors, Marvalene Hughes, now president of Dillard University; Jane Canney, now of the University of St. Thomas; Steven Baker at the University of Minnesota; and my current supervisor, Gerald Rinehart. I am especially grateful to my circle of colleagues and friends who serve parents at institutions throughout the United States as well as to my own family. I also must express my appreciation to the parents I work with every day in my job.

Published online in Wiley InterScience
(www.interscience.wiley.com) • DOI: 10.1002/aehe.3306

Overview

PARENTAL INVOLVEMENT. This term, previously reserved for the K–12 lexicon, has recently migrated into the vocabulary of college administrators. Since the late 1990s, colleges and universities have noted a cultural shift in the relationship between most parents and their traditional-age college students. This new relationship is puzzling to college staff and administrators, partly because it does not reflect the experience of their own college years but mostly because it affects the relationship of each party—students and parents—to the college or university itself. The role of parents as a critical secondary audience has introduced a new dynamic in providing communications, events, and services for families. As we consider the continuing role of parents in the lives of their college-age students, we seek to define the issues, the questions, and the relationships that the phenomenon of parental involvement has raised for students, parents, and the institution.

Introduction to the Monograph

This report is divided into three main sections: theoretical grounding, student identity, and implications. The first section, theoretical grounding of parental involvement, looks at the reasons parents today are more likely to be involved in their students' lives and then reviews the literature of K–12 education and compares that information with what exists on the transition to college and higher education. It considers the current student development and higher education literature and the tension that exists between them with regard to separation-individuation and attachment theory. This section goes on to look

---

at the institution's role in the relationship between college students and parents and how it has shifted over time. It also specifically considers the question of whether college students are children or adults, as this perspective affects the definition of the parent-student relationship.

The second section takes into account the individual variables of student identity that may affect the relationship between parents and students. We review the literature on parent-student relationships in terms of the effects of gender, race, and socioeconomic class, paying particular attention to parents' educational level and focusing on first-generation students. We examine the literature, particularly from K–12 education, that shows that parents' participation in schooling varies by social class. We look at research showing that support and encouragement are key factors in the literature on college access, which indicates that the level of support for attending college seems to be inextricably linked with social class. In considering the parent-student relationship and college access, we also look at upper-middle-class students and their approach to the college admissions process, especially at highly selective institutions. These students have involved parents who want their child to attend the "best college" and often serve as the source of pressure for students in the admissions process because of their desire for a return on their investment, both the future investment from tuition dollars and the past financial cost of raising a child (Karen, 2002; Mathews, 1998; McDonough, 1997; Robbins, 2006).

The final section comprises implications for both policy and practice. We include the history of and current frameworks for parent relations programs. Increasingly, colleges and universities are debating the value and the cost of providing services and programming for the parents of their students. Data from studies conducted in 2005 and 2007 show that schools that provide parent services are expanding their efforts beyond one or two annual events to include regular communications, dispersal of student development information, inclusion of parents as members of advisory groups and as volunteers or mentors, and solicitation of funds. We look at ways that parents have been included in the discussion as schools address significant campus issues such as student drinking, physical and mental health, finances, career development, campus safety, and preparation for off-campus living. This section also provides information on how institutions provide information to parents as a way to deliver or reinforce important messages to students.

We conclude this publication with recommendations for administrators in higher education as well as student development faculty. We also suggest areas for further research. The appendix includes literature and Web-based resources for those looking for more information on the topic of parental involvement in higher education.

Defining Parental Involvement

What does parental involvement mean in the context of higher education? According to Karen Levin Coburn, a student affairs practitioner and co-author of *Letting Go: A Parents' Guide to Understanding the College Years,* the contemporary parent of a college student is often described through examples of extreme behavior: contacting the college late at night to report a mouse discovered in a daughter's room, complaining about a roommate who snores, expressing anger over a grade on a paper "my son worked so hard on" (Coburn, 2006, p. 9). Dubbed by the media as "helicopter parents," this subpopulation of overly involved mothers and fathers has come to represent all parents of college students.

The popular image of college parents is the mother drafting to-do lists, checking grades, reviewing bank statements, and logging into her child's e-mail with the student's personal password (ABC News, 2005). Human interest stories, positioned on the front pages of major media like *The New York Times,* present parents as being ever-present as they check in with cell phones and e-mail, edit their student's paper, purchase their student's textbooks, review course syllabi, help students find summer internships and jobs, and even guide their postcollege career searches (Kantrowitz and Tyre, 2006; Lewin, 2003; Shellenbarger, 2005). These "kamikaze parents," as one company's director of college relations calls them, have even been contacting hiring managers to dispute students' pay packages and renegotiate them (Shellenbarger, 2006).

The term *helicopter parent* has quickly become part of the American educational vocabulary. The term is now included in *Wikipedia,* the online encyclopedia edited by the general public. Subspecies of helicopter parents are now emerging. For example, the Black Hawk parent—a helicopter parent whose behavior is not only excessive but in some cases unethical (Wikipedia, 2007)—joins lawnmower parents (mowing down anything in their way), submarine parents (hidden below the surface and popping up to attack when things go wrong), and stealth missiles (arriving under the radar and destroying any obstacles in their path). As a result of the media coverage of parental involvement, this image has become familiar to the general public, including parents themselves.

But is the image of the hovering helicopter parent the most accurate portrayal of the relationship between parents and their college-bound or college-attending students? Although the media have largely grouped parents into the broad category of "helicopter parents," it is important for both administrators and researchers to remember that this image only represents an extreme group, and parents—and their individual relationships with their students—are as varied as the students themselves. The media's front-page stories and the dean's office water cooler tales of parents' behavior would have us believe that all parents of all college students act in this manner. And although parental involvement certainly takes these forms, these images do not tell the whole story.

To assess parental involvement in its true form, we need to consider what parental involvement really looks like. What does it mean for a parent to be involved? Is it inherently bad? Has our educational system, or our society, changed sufficiently in recent years to justify a need for personal advocacy for college students? What are the effects of the parent-student relationship on both students and parents? What are its effects on the college? Is the definition of parental involvement standard for all college students, or does it differ based on specific factors, in particular, socioeconomic class, parental level of education, and cultural background?

Many colleges and universities have found that parental involvement has its positive points. Parents can be effective partners, reinforcing the messages that schools are attempting to deliver about mental health concerns, retention, graduation, and responsible financial management. Parents can add value to institutional messages by reminding the student of a family history of alcoholism or chronic health conditions and by detecting problems long before they become apparent to anyone on campus. This partnership between the college or university and parents can result in healthy, positive choices and outcomes for students. Do parents who are more invested in their students' lives and in the institution sound intrinsically evil? It is important to remember that some families are not at all involved in their students' lives.

In this monograph, we have formulated our own definition of parental involvement. For our purposes, the phenomenon of parental involvement includes parents' showing interest in the lives of their students in college, gaining more information about college, knowing when and how to appropriately provide encouragement and guidance to their student connecting with the institution, and potentially retaining that institutional connection beyond the college years. We do not think this involvement is inherently wrong. We support parental involvement in the sense that it helps parents understand the higher education they are paying for, helps them understand college students' development, provides support for students, and, increasingly, supplements institutional budgets (in certain cases). This monograph is not, then, a discussion about helicopter parents but an in-depth look at the relationship between parents and their traditional-age college students and how this changing relationship affects the connection of each of these parties to the institution.

Reasons for Parental Involvement

WHAT DO WE KNOW ABOUT PARENTAL INVOLVEMENT and the emerging cultural shift in parent-student relationships? First, parents and students are talking to each other more frequently—an average of more than 1.5 times per day (Junco and Mastrodicasa, 2007) and using multiple technologies. According to the 2007 National Survey of Student Engagement, seven out of ten students said that they communicated "very often" with at least one parent or guardian during the academic year. It was more popular to communicate with electronic media than face to face (National Survey of Student Engagement, 2007).

Moreover, students are not troubled by the level of involvement they have with their parents. According to data released by the Higher Education Research Institute at the University of California, Los Angeles, most students perceive their parents' involvement to be "just right" (Higher Education Research Institute, 2008). A Student Health 101 survey came to the same conclusion, noting that 83 percent of students said their parents are "involved just the right amount" in their lives (Roarty, 2007, p. 9). Moreover, the topics that students discuss most with their parents just may be topics about which parents should have at least some input: finances, health and well-being, and career planning (College Parents of America, 2007). Discussions may change over the course of a college career: at one institution, parents of freshmen and sophomores report that their students are most frequently turning to them for information and advice on health and safety issues and academics; parents of juniors get the most questions about finances; and parents of seniors are most often asked for advice on career planning (Savage, 2006). Conversations may also vary depending on whom the student is talking to. According to the 2007 data from the National Survey of Student Engagement, students were likely to talk to their mothers about personal issues, academic performance, and family matters. Academic performance was the most common discussion topic with fathers (National Survey of Student Engagement, 2007).

Among some faculty, staff, and administrators, this level of parental involvement has been seen as troublesome, based on concerns that parental involvement interferes with their students' development as autonomous individuals. Indeed at some colleges and universities, administrators must actively fend off parental involvement, even to the point of assigning "parent bouncers" to prevent parents from accompanying students to course registration at orientation (Shellenbarger, 2005). At other institutions, however, administrators have determined that if parents are going to be involved, someone should define and direct that involvement. To that end, they have introduced parent relations offices to supplement parent orientation programs, provide communications directed to parents, schedule family-focused events, and respond to parents' concerns throughout the academic year and the student's college experience.

The focus of the conversation about the effects of parental involvement is just starting to shift. Results of the 2007 National Survey of Student Engagement showed that students who frequently talk with their parents and follow their advice are likely to participate more often in college activities and are more satisfied with their college experience (National Survey of Student Engagement, 2007). Previously, as educators looked for research to explain and guide this new phenomenon of parental involvement, they found little in the way of scholarly, academic literature. What they found instead are the theories of Neil Howe and William Strauss. In their book, *Millennials Rising: The Next Great Generation* (2000), Howe and Strauss describe the attitudes and behaviors of this generation of students, born during or after 1982, who were first noted as the "Babies on Board" of the early Reagan years. The authors followed up in 2003 with *Millennials Go to College,* which advises campus professionals on how they should respond to the arrival of these students on campus, led by the high school graduates of 2000.

According to Howe and Strauss (2003), Millennial students share seven core traits. One of the most significant characteristics is that they are "sheltered."

For Millennials, "the edifice of parental care has been like a castle that keeps getting new bricks added" (p. 176). Parents of Millennials have been highly safety and security conscious since the birth of this new generation, resulting in Millennials feeling that their parents will protect them—and perhaps over-protect them. Overall, Howe and Strauss say that the "generation gap" between parents and children is narrowing as Millennials and their parents maintain a significant closeness. According to the parents Howe and Strauss (2003) surveyed, Millennial children disclose extensive information about their daily lives, including the topics of sex, drugs, and alcohol, far beyond what the Boomers and GenXers admit sharing with their own parents. Howe and Strauss (2000) say that two-thirds of today's teenagers report that their parents are "in touch" with their lives and that it is "easy" to talk to their parents (p. 187).

As generational theory pervades the conversation about today's family involvement, some important questions must be considered: Why do Howe and Strauss's theories dominate the discourse on parental involvement? Are there other explanations? Why is a source that draws its research primarily from anecdotes and even Howe and Strauss's own children (Howe and Strauss are each a parent to two Millennials) so popular? And what happens when we look at the first group of Millennials' parents, the Baby Boomers, and con-sider the parents who are now showing up on campuses, the GenXers?

In his review of *Millennials Rising: The Next Great Generation,* David Brooks, author of his own piece on contemporary young people called *The Organization Kid,* says that Howe and Strauss's work is a "very good bad book" (Brooks, 2000). Even though Howe and Strauss make huge generalizations— including some broad statements that Brooks says might make you want to "hurl [the book] against the wall," he also acknowledges that their book has some merit. "This is not a good book, if by good you mean the kind of book in which the authors have rigorously sifted the evidence and carefully sup-ported their assertions with data. . . . It's stuffed with interesting nuggets. It's brightly written. And if you get away from the generational mumbo jumbo, it illuminates changes that really do seem to be taking place" (Brooks, 2000). Perhaps Brooks is accurate in that Howe and Strauss's style and their identifi-cation of change explain why the concept of Millennials has become so pop-ular. Even though the research is not empirically or scholarly sound, maybe those who work closely with today's traditional-age college students embrace it because it rings true.

The Millennials cannot possibly tell the whole story of parental involvement, however. We believe generation is certainly a factor in the phenomenon of parental involvement, but it is just one. The next few chapters help to provide those grappling with the phenomenon of parental involvement with multiple ways of understanding it, what it is, and why it is happening, rather than just the simple concept of a generational shift. They also illustrate different aspects of the parent-student relationship in an attempt to avoid the broad generalizations that have been used to describe this generation thus far.

Based on research, the study of various theorists, communication with parent program professionals, and interactions with parents and students, we have identified five primary factors that may contribute to the phenomenon of parental involvement: generation, cost of college, use of technology, changes in parenting, and demographics. We believe these five factors are the dominant reasons for parents' increased levels of involvement, although through this monograph we investigate not just the reasons for but also the effects of involvement.

Generation

Howe and Strauss focus on students in terms of generation. According to Strauss and Howe (1991), generations are people moving through time, and each group or generation of people presents a distinctive sense of self. Year of birth is what determines the identification of a generation—a "peer personality" or set of collective traits and attitudes. Strauss and Howe argue that a recurring cycle comprises four distinct types of peer personalities—Idealist, Reactive, Civic, and Adaptive (p. 35)—which correspond to the physical age of the members of the generation during different periods of history. The four cycles repeat over and over in the same sequence. The latest group is the Millennials, who represent the Civic peer group (Strauss and Howe, 1991). According to Strauss and Howe, a Civic generation grows up as youths who are very protected, experiencing coming of age during a secular crisis and becoming heroic and achieving young adults.

Helen Lefkowitz Horowitz (1987) also writes about college culture and generations. In *Campus Life,* she describes the ways that college students have defined themselves from the end of the eighteenth century until the time her book was written, 1987. In the broader college culture, however, she focuses on student subcultures. According to Horowitz, both higher education historians and the American public typically have used the term "college life" to refer to an undergraduate subculture, presumably shared by all students. Actually, however, college life has been the reality of only a minority of students whom she calls "college men and women" (p. x).

Horowitz emphasizes that undergraduates of the traditional four-year residential college have not shared one student subculture but instead have been divided among competing subcultures. These subcultures include the conventional "college men and women," who find themselves at the center of college culture, usually members of fraternal organizations; "outsiders," who oppose the majority and are excluded from these organizations; and "rebels," who are vocal outsiders. Over the course of the history of American higher education, women and other groups typically excluded from higher education such as racial and religious minority groups have been part of both the outsider and rebel groups (Horowitz, 1987).

Certainly we can learn about trends in student culture from studying generation, but by focusing on all students in a generational group, Howe and Strauss may be overlooking student subcultures that, as Horowitz says, may better define who students are. Are "college men and women" only one segment of the college student population after all, and by generalizing are we placing values and characteristics on all students that may apply only to a certain group? Although we can learn much from generational theory, we have to be cautious about characteristics applied to an entire population.

Similarly, the discussion of college parents in recent years has focused on Baby Boomer parents, those born between 1946 and the early 1960s. Now that we are seeing GenX parents bringing their students to college, administrators and practitioners are wondering what changes to expect from a new generation of mothers and fathers. Like with students, however, we believe the most critical factors are not purely generational but lie in the segments and subcultures of the families we are seeing.

Cost of College

College costs have been rising, and they continue to increase. The average comprehensive cost (published charges for tuition, room, board, and fees) at private four-year colleges and universities has risen at an average rate of 2.9 percent each year for the past ten years, after adjusting for inflation (College Board, 2007b). The average comprehensive cost at public four-year institutions has increased by 4.4 percent each year, again after adjusting for inflation. The average cost at four-year institutions during the 2007–2008 academic year was $13,589 for resident students at public colleges and $32,307 for students at private colleges (College Board, 2007b). Just ten years earlier, for the 1997–1998 school year, the average comprehensive cost for four-year institutions was $9,657 for resident students at four-year public colleges and $25,031 for resident students at four-year private colleges (prices given in constant dollars) (College Board, 2007b). And there is no sign that college costs will come down any time soon.

Along with the rise in college costs has been a shift over time in terms of who pays for college and whether higher education is seen as a public or private good. Costs for college borne students and their parents have increased significantly as a result of factors such as decreasing state funding at public colleges and the recycling of tuition dollars into financial aid at private colleges (Johnstone, 2005). These costs for all college students and parents are high, but they are considered to be the highest for relatively affluent families at high-cost private institutions (Johnstone, 2005). It is the families themselves who are helping to finance the education of their children and bearing the burden of increased costs. A significant amount of this parental financing comes from borrowing money through loans. For example, over the past decade the number of parents of undergraduate students who have taken a Parent Loan for Undergraduate Students (PLUS) increased by 92 percent, while the average amount of the loan increased by 39 percent (College Board, 2007c).

College graduates with bachelor's degrees earn twice as much as their peers who have only high school diplomas; over a lifetime the earnings gap between a high school diploma and a bachelor's degree is more than $1 million (College Board, 2007a). These facts may not be enough to justify this investment for today's college students and their families, however. They are still left questioning the cost of a college education. Parents today expect a more concrete, tangible return on their investment such as contemporary housing options, high levels of technology, and a clear path to a career upon graduation. From the vantage point of the institution, pressure is increasing to provide students and their families with this tangible return. Some colleges and universities have begun to treat students and families primarily as consumers, a contractual relationship where payment of tuition and fees guarantees receipt of certain services from the college (Bickel and Lake, 1997; Fass, Morrill, and Mount, 1986). Geiger (2004) claims that the market has driven institutions to become student centered as they compete for students, which has led to an increase in the amenities provided to students to ensure that they enjoy a high level of comfort at college. Many students and parent have come to expect these amenities (Geiger, 2004).

Use of Technology

During the lifetime of today's college students, technology has changed the way most of us communicate. The use of technology, in particular cellular phones, the Internet, e-mail, text messaging, and instant messaging, has risen. Students use all these technologies, most of them for communicating with parents. Students talk to their parents on cell phones frequently, far more frequently than most college staff did during their own college years. Richard Mullendore, a professor at the University of Georgia has called the cell phone the world's longest umbilical cord (Shellenbarger, 2005). According to a survey by Junco and Mastrodicasa (2007), students reported speaking with their parents an average of 1.5 times per day, and 57.6 percent of the time it was the students who initiated the calls. It is possible that student-parent communications are as much an interference in parents' lives as in students' lives. Although most conversations occurred while parents were at home, many occurred when parents were at work or driving their cars (Junco and Mastrodicasa, 2007).

In their survey, Junco and Mastrodicasa (2007) found the most popular topics that parents and students reported talking about were simply checking in, academic success, and social life. How students communicate with different family members may reflect the individuals, however. A student may talk to her mother on her cell phone, text with her little sister, and send letters to her grandmother.

In terms of other forms of technology, and the Internet in particular, college students today use computers to communicate at a higher rate than others in the general population. In *The Internet Goes to College: How Students Are Living in the Future with Today's Technology* (2002), 86 percent of college students had been online, compared with 59 percent of all Americans; 72 percent of college students checked their e-mail daily, while only 52 percent of all Americans with Internet access did so; and 26 percent of college students used instant messaging on an average day, compared with 12 percent of all Internet users (Pew Internet and American Life Project, 2002). Unlike the previous generation, using technology to communicate when they go to college is nothing new for today's students.

Students communicate with their parents by e-mail regularly. Trice (2002) found that "the development of e-mail has increased communication between students and parents enormously" (p. 327). In a qualitative study of forty-eight first-year students (twenty-four men and twenty-four women) who were eighteen or nineteen years old, students were asked about their communication with their parents via e-mail (Trice, 2002). The content of the students' e-mails to parents was coded primarily for the issues of academics, social issues, and finances. Students in the study had an average of 6.03 e-mail contacts with parents per week (Trice, 2002). During periods of academic stress such as exam time, contacts with parents increased. These students reported, however, that the nature of their contact with parents was not necessarily to seek advice. Students simply had more contact with parents during weeks that were stressful than not stressful.

When considering students' use of technology to communicate with their parents, we need to keep in mind that the use of technology between students (and parents) of different cultural and socioeconomic groups may differ. In a study of 272,821 first-year college students, Latinos and African Americans communicated via e-mail less than whites and Asian Americans, when income levels were controlled (Sax, Ceja, and Teranishi, 2001). In addition, according to a 2004 study based on census data, the Department of Commerce National Telecommunications and Information Administration (NTIA) found that just 37.2 percent of Latinos and 45.6 percent of African Americans used the Internet, while 65.1 percent of whites and 63.1 percent of Asian Americans did. Only 12.6 percent of Latinos and 14.2 percent of African Americans lived in households with broadband Internet access, compared with 25.7 percent of whites and 34.2 percent of Asian Americans. According to the NTIA study, Internet use and access to a broadband Internet connection at home is a linear function of income—the lower one's income, the lower one's use of the Internet and the lower the likelihood that he or she can access it from home (U.S. Department of Commerce, 2004; Junco and Mastrodicasa, 2007).

When working with families and implementing communications, administrators should consider how the use of technology may differ among population groups. At the same time it is important to question assumptions about these groups. When the University of Minnesota's parent program looked into a perception that low-income rural families would not be likely to have the same level of Internet access as suburban families, they found that their rural families tended to farm for a living and that they had long been using computers and the Internet to record and report their crops. Internet access may have been slower in rural areas, but it was available. A similar broad-based concern about parents of first-generation American students proved to be equally unfounded. Many first-generation families were using the Internet, sometimes at libraries or community centers, to read online news stories of home and to communicate with friends and families back home. In some cases, language was a barrier, but access was not.

Technology is a primary method of communication for today's families. Online polls conducted by Calvin College's parent program show that technology is simply part of a family's daily routine. When parents were asked how frequently they check their e-mail inbox, more than half (58.5 percent) said three or more times a day. Fewer than 10 percent said they do not check their e-mail daily. When asked how their student most frequently contacts the parent, only 3.7 percent cited landline phone as the most frequent communication method, and only 1.6 percent mentioned in-person contact (Calvin College,

2007). Although some families still maintain more traditional communication styles—a once-a-week phone call or the occasional snail-mail card or package—for most students and their parents today, e-mail, calls on the cell phone, instant messaging, or texting is a daily activity.

Changes in Parenting

The twentieth century has been dubbed "the century of the child" (Hulbert, 2003; Stearns, 2003). Public sources of advice about parenting first became available in the early 1900s and attained popularity during the 1920s (Hulbert, 2003; Stearns, 2003). In general, the twentieth century signified a shift in adult-child relationships, and those new relationships were marked by parents' anxiety. In the early 1900s, parents began to worry about things such as their children's posture, which morphed into how early the child learned to walk or became potty trained. Parents' worries have been amplified as time has passed and new things to worry about have emerged. They eventually dropped the concern over how tall a child stood, and they decided children learned to walk or use the toilet at their own pace. Instead they began to worry about safety seats for cars, helmets for bicycles, and mouth guards for Little Leaguers, and more recently they have focused on their child's body mass index or how much time the child spends on video games (Stearns, 2003).

During the later part of the twentieth century, families experienced significant changes in parent-child contact. According to a 2001 study, the amount of time children spent with both parents increased 25 percent between 1981 and 1997 (Hofferth and Sandberg, 2001). Parents were aware that they were devoting more time to their children and that it was intentional. Parents said that they limited their children's use of playpens because playpens reduced the need and the opportunity for direct parent-child interaction. The study also noted that children were watching less television. Instead they participated in more sports (Hofferth and Sandberg, 2001). During the 1980s and 1990s, the childhood years of today's college students, the image of the "frenzied soccer moms and dads" shuttling their children from one scheduled activity to another emerged (Stearns, 2003, p. 9). The "postmodern parenthood" who managed overscheduled kids became dominant (p. 9).

Brooks describes this parenting style and the lifestyle of highly scheduled children who attend elite colleges in *The Organization Kid*. According to Brooks (2001), the students currently in college likely spent "their afternoons and weekends shuttling from one skill-enhancing activity to the next" (p. 4). They have spent the majority of their lives "in structured, adult-organized activities" (p. 5). Parental anxiety often stems from a fear that their children will not succeed. As Brooks points out, this type of parenting is largely a class-based phenomenon. Although these trends are dominant themes in modern parenting and we can better understand many of today's college students from learning about them, they tend to refer only to the behaviors of parents in the middle and upper-middle classes.

For children from lower-income and socioeconomic status groups, contemporary childhood looks different. Poor and working-class parents want the best for their children, just like middle-class parents. But tasks such as putting food on the table, paying for housing, protecting students from the problems in unsafe neighborhoods, arranging for health care, cleaning clothes, and getting children into bed for a good night's rest are all challenging when economic resources are scarce (Lareau, 2003). These parents, unlike middle- and upper-middle-class parents, however, do not consider developing their children through attendance at organized activities. Instead, children themselves have more control over what they do with their "free time." In general, these parents have a different construction of the role of parenthood and see a clear boundary between children and adults (Lareau, 2003). Unfortunately, as the educational system tends to privilege the values of the middle class, these children may be at a disadvantage at school compared with their peers of higher socioeconomic classes (Lareau, 1987, 2003).

Demographics

Data from 1971 to 2000 for the Cooperative Institutional Research Program's freshman survey shows trends in the composition of freshmen classes at the most selective institutions by parental income levels (Astin and Oseguera, 2004). Over this period of time, representation of students from high-income families increased steadily (an increase from 46 percent to 55 percent of the entering class) and representation of students from middle-income levels decreased steadily (a decrease from 41 percent to 33 percent of the entering class). The representation of low-income students at this type of institution changed little, with enrollment holding steady between 9 percent and 13 percent of entering freshmen (Astin and Oseguera, 2004).

When viewed in terms of parents' education level, the composition of first-year students over this time has changed significantly. For example, in 1971, the entering classes of the most selective institutions had approximately equal numbers of students whose parents had never attended college (25 percent) and students whose parents both had college degrees (28 percent) (Astin and Oseguera, 2004). At the most selective institutions in recent years, college students with highly educated parents have outnumbered first-generation college students by six to one (62 percent versus 9 percent in 2000) (Astin and Oseguera, 2004).

Although this increase in students whose parents went to college is more prevalent at the most selective institutions, the number of first-generation college students has diminished over all levels of institutional selectivity (Astin and Oseguera, 2004). This trend as well as the increase in students from higher income levels, the decrease in students from middle income levels, and the constancy of students from low income levels could have a number of implications, not only for college access but also for the role of parents in higher education. If parents have gone to college themselves, they may approach the educational system differently from those parents who did not attend college. We believe that the increase in the population of students with highly educated parents affects student-parent relationship, especially the relationship among student, parent, and institution.

The number of first-generation students who attend a particular institution is often determined by how selective the institution is. American higher education is stratified according to socioeconomic status (parents' income and education level) even more distinctly than it was thirty years ago (Astin and Oseguera, 2004). More than 60 percent of students in the entering classes of the most selective institutions have parents who both have a college degree. In comparison, one-third of the students at schools of middle selectivity and only about 18 percent of students in the least selective colleges have parents who are described as highly educated (both have a college degree) (Astin and Oseguera, 2004).

In assessing demographics and the relationship between college students and their parents, another demographic factor is important to consider. Although this publication focuses on traditional-age college students and their parents, it is important to remember that about half of all undergraduates do not fall between ages nineteen and twenty-three *(Chronicle of Higher Education,* 2007–2008). Of these "nontraditional" students, many are actually parents themselves. Although this monograph does not address this issue directly, we urge administrators to consider the needs of this population and how best to serve them. For those students who are parents themselves as well as of traditional age, the dynamic and relationship between student and parent is even more complicated.

Theoretical Grounding

WHEN EXAMINING THE LITERATURE and research on parental involvement, one must include K–12 literature along with the research about college access programs that are designed to help low-income students gain admission to and prepare for college. In these access programs, the role of parents in students' development is more clearly defined and readily embraced than in the higher education literature on college student development. More important, that parental role in K–12 sets the pattern—through its success—for parental behaviors that are often viewed as intrusive at the college level.

What should the role of a parent be in a student's education? What are the effects of this role? The answers to these questions are mixed and conflicting. A tension exists between the effects of parental involvement in the literature discussing K–12 education, which promotes involvement, as opposed to the literature from the field of higher education, which tends to support individuation and a student's development of autonomy, specifically through separation from parents and family. A tension also exists in the body of literature on college students' psychological development as it relates to conclusions about the college student–parent relationship and its effects on students' identity formation.

The role of parents in the psychological development of college students is unclear. The tension surrounding this topic in the literature is the very conflict that administrators have expressed when working with college students and parents: they are wary of the potential effects of increased parental involvement. Many of those who work with students are concerned that parents prevent students from becoming individuals and developing along traditional lines like the many generations of students before them (Savage, 2003). Will parental involvement ultimately help or hinder students' development?

K–12 Literature

The literature on K–12 education is important because most of the literature on the framework of parental involvement comes from the K–12 context. Although not much research has been undertaken on the effects of parental involvement on traditional-age college students, the effects of the parent-child relationship on students from early childhood through high school are better known. Admittedly the developmental goals for high school and college students are different, and they require different types and amounts of parental involvement, in the same way that developmental goals differ in elementary and high school. For all students—early childhood, elementary school, middle school, and high school— the literature indicates that high levels of parental involvement make a significant positive difference in personal and academic growth.

Parental involvement throughout the K–12 years has been linked to such positive outcomes as higher grades, success in school, higher standardized test scores, higher self-esteem, more social competence, reduced substance use, aspirations for college, enrollment in college, and participation in out-of-school programs (Harvard Family Research Project, 2007). In the K–12 arena, parental (or more broadly family) involvement can be defined by three main processes: (1) parenting, which considers the values and attitudes that parents have, which in turn affect how they raise their children; (2) home-school relationships, which reflect the role of the institution in the parent-child relationship—the formal and information connections between the family and the school; and (3) responsibility for learning, that is, parents' emphasis on activities that promote the student's growth, both socially and academically (Harvard Family Research Project, 2007).

Unlike higher education, standards for parental involvement in K–12 education are clearly understood and clearly articulated. Parental involvement is an important component of the No Child Left Behind Act of 2001, which has had an influence on the education of today's traditional-age college students. A U.S. Department of Education publication designed to help parents of K–12 students understand No Child Left Behind suggests the following actions for parents:

> Work with your child's teacher and school to keep the lines of com-
> munication open. Partner with the teacher to enhance the academic
> success and social well being of your child. Attend parent-teacher
> meetings and stay informed about your child's academic progress.
> Discuss with your child's teacher what you can do at home to help
> your child. Go on field trips with your child's class and volunteer
> to help the teacher in the classroom, on the playground or at spe-
> cial events. Talk with your child daily about school. Ask your child
> what he or she learned that day. Ask how the day went, and ask
> about your child's friends. Review your child's homework each
> evening, and consult homework Web sites if available. Be sure that
> your child completes all of his or her assignments [U.S. Department
> of Education, 2007, p. 5].

What causes a parent to be involved? According to Hoover-Dempsey and Sandler (1997), three main factors cause parents to become involved in their children's education: the parent's construction of his or her role in the child's life, the parent's sense of efficacy for helping the child succeed in school, and the institutional role or the general invitations and opportunities for parental involvement presented by both the child and the school.

The role of the institution in the parent-student relationship is key. The degree to which a parent is involved depends not only on the relationship with his or her particular student but also with the student's school and the extent to which parents are included and encouraged to participate in their child's educational process (Hoover-Dempsey and Sandler, 1997). What does this relationship mean for higher education? If K–12 institutions are encouraging parental involvement and telling parents what involvement is, how does it trans- late to the college years? How do parents know what their role is in higher edu- cation? Is it still the institution's role to define appropriate involvement for parents? In higher education, we are just beginning to formulate our definition of the term "parent involvement" and what the parent-student relationship means in the context of institutions of higher education as we learn more about the current phenomenon.

The answers to these questions are influenced by the parents' socioeconomic status. The discourse about trends in parenting and institutional standards for parental involvement is most frequently based on middle-class behaviors. Parent-school interactions and the degree to which parents meet the standards for involvement are affected by parents' class status (Lareau, 1987).

College Student Development: Separation-Individuation

The higher education literature that describes the student-parent relationship is remarkably different from the K–12 literature that describes this relationship. The prevailing theory about college students' development was that acquiring autonomy and individuation were necessary components of emotional adjustment to college. The reasoning was that students with a better sense of themselves as individuals would be better able to perform the new tasks required of them as college students such as waking up on time, attending classes, arranging one's course schedule, and dealing with the dynamics of the college social world (Mattanah, Brand, and Hancock, 2004). Separation-individuation is most frequently described as a developmental process that begins with separation from parents to achieve self-definition and the ability to function autonomously (Mattanah, Brand, and Hancock, 2004; Rice, 1992). Erikson (1968) used this theory of individuation to represent the central task of adolescence (see also Kenny and Donaldson, 1991). It later became the prevailing theory used to predict the likelihood of adjustment to college during the 1970s and 1980s (Mattanah, Brand, and Hancock, 2004).

Chickering uses this theory as the basis for development of autonomy in *Education and Identity,* first written in 1969 and revised with Reisser in 1993. According to Chickering and Reisser (1993), a necessary developmental process for students is learning to function with emotional independence or without the need for reassurance, affection, or approval. Movement toward this state begins with separation from parents (Chickering and Reisser, 1993).

In the more recent version of *Education and Identity*, the vector of "autonomy" has been changed to "moving through autonomy to interdependence" to place greater emphasis on "respecting the autonomy of others and looking for ways to give and take with an ever-expanding circle of friends" (Chickering and Reisser, 1993, p. 48); however, the description of the vector and its process remains basically unchanged from the 1969 model (Taub, 1997).

Secure Attachment

Attachment theory in the context of higher education emerged as a competing theory to separation-individuation in the 1990s. Attachment theory challenges the traditional implications of separation-individuation by suggesting that, for students leaving home, having parents as a secure base may actually support rather than threaten the development of competence and autonomy (Kenny and Donaldson, 1992). The implications of this theory may affect how we view the relationship between parents and students. According to Kenny and Rice (1995), the attachment model suggests that calling home to talk with family or discuss a concern with parents may actually be examples of healthy behavior rather than acts that are cause for concern.

Human development research has contributed to the body of knowledge about these "leaving home stages." Bowlby originally conceptualized attachment theory in 1973 to explain the distress infants and young children experienced when separated from their parents (Schwartz and Buboltz, 2004). It is based on the idea that an infant's ability to explore the world is a direct result of having a "secure base" (Schwartz and Buboltz, 2004; Vivona, 2000). According to Bowlby, individuals who are both emotionally stable and self-reliant are likely to have parents who are available to provide support when needed while simultaneously encouraging autonomy (Kenny and Rice, 1995). In *A Secure Base: Parent-Child Attachment and Healthy Human Development*, Bowlby defines attachment as "any type of behavior that results in a person attaining or maintaining proximity to some other clearly identified individual who is conceived as better able to cope with the world" (Bowlby, 1988, p. 26). According to Bowlby, the attachment relationship is most obvious when the subject is frightened, fatigued, or sick and then is calmed through comfort and caregiving. At other times, however, the specific behavior is less evident. To know that an attachment figure is available for support can provide a strong sense of security that encourages the subject to value and continue the relationship. Attachment behavior is most obvious in early childhood, but in adolescence, attachment takes the form of autonomy and independence with the maintenance of warm and supportive relationships (Sorokou and Weissbrod, 2005). Moreover, Bowlby (1988) says that it can be observed throughout the life cycle, especially in times of emergency.

When the theory of attachment is applied in the context of college, it challenges traditional notions of separation-individuation espoused by student affairs personnel. A number of human development theorists support this concept of attachment to describe more accurately the developmental relationship between college students and their parents. According to Kenny (1987), for example, secure attachment relationships offer support in times of stress, allowing students to confidently explore their new environment. Therefore, the process of leaving home for college students can be conceptualized as a new and stress-raising situation in which the availability of parents may support rather than threaten a student's development of competence and autonomy (Kenny, 1987). Rather than needing a defined separation or break from parents, students under this scenario may actually benefit from regular parental contact and support.

Sorokou and Weissbrod (2005) define attachment specifically in terms of the type of contact students have with their parents. Their research measured need and non-need-based contact patterns (such as telephoning, e-mailing, and visiting) between adolescents, during their first year of college, and with their parents. They define need-based contact as "support-seeking behaviors at times of need" and non-need-based contact as "behaviors for the purpose of touching base and maintaining contact" (p. 226). They found that a positive relationship existed between perceived quality of attachment and frequency of students' contact with parents, both need and non–need based. Moreover, in secure attachment relationships the relationship was two sided, with the non-need-based contact initiated by parents as well as students. Frequency of student-initiated need-based contact was also positively related to students' reports of parent-initiated non-need-based contact (Sorokou and

Weissbrod, 2005). In the theory of attachment, therefore, student-parent contacts such as calling one another to "check in" may be just as significant to college students as contacting parents during times of trouble. These findings are consistent with those of Trice (2002) discussed earlier, that students contacted parents often by e-mail, just to check in rather than to ask for help or advice.

Attachment and Gender

Some theorists argue that the relational nature of the attachment model supports the idea that women are more attached to their parents than men and that attachment theory may better reflect the experiences of female college students. According to Gilligan (1993), the relationship between self and others does indeed differ along gender lines, with males favoring a process of separation and females favoring a process of attachment. For women, relationships are the main focus of attention and concern (Gilligan, 1993). Because they are socialized into feminine roles, girls develop a self defined by relationships to others as well as a concern for sustaining these relationships (Kenny and Rice, 1995). Allen and Stoltenberg (1995) also suggest it may be more important for women to retain close ties with family while in college than men.

Although some research supports the idea that gender makes a difference in attachment relationships, other theorists conclude that gender is not a factor. Lapsley, Rice, and Fitzgerald (1990), for example, found no significant difference in attachment to parents in their study of adolescent attachment to parents and peers. In addition, Mattanah, Brand, and Hancock (2004) suggest that simply having a history of secure attachment would mediate the effects of separation-individuation and therefore lead to greater adjustment to college. They found that secure attachment was associated with adjustment for both men and women, which challenges the idea that men strive for separation from relationships, while women strive for separation in relationships.

Combining Theories

According to Schwartz and Buboltz (2004), although the concepts of psychological separation and attachment (as defined by Bowlby) appear to disagree, they are not mutually exclusive but in equilibrium. This balance between attachment and separation may include a degree of conflict with both parents (Schwartz and Buboltz, 2004; Bowlby, 1969). Therefore, according to Schwartz and Buboltz (2004) and attachment theory, emotional connection and contact between parents and colleges students is healthy, but so is some conflict. It is ultimately both separation-individuation and attachment that lead to positive emotional adjustment.

Schultheiss and Blustein (1994) examined both the variables of separation-individuation and attachment, believing that separation-individuation may actually come about most successfully through the context of adolescent-parent connectedness. In other words, students who are securely attached to their parents might have an easier time negotiating the process of individuating and adjusting to a new environment. In their results, they found that the combined effects of separation-individuation and attachment were a predictor of college student development for women and of college student adjustment for men (Schultheiss and Blustein, 1994).

Mattanah, Brand, and Hancock (2004) also found that the process of individuation was actually facilitated by the presence of secure relationships with parents when parents were supportive of their students in college. In addition, for Josselson (1987) the definition of separation-individuation includes elements of attachment theory. According to Josselson (1987), the problem of separating "is the problem of not only becoming different, but of becoming different and maintaining connection at the same time" (p. 171). Therefore, even though it is necessary for students to become distinct individuals from their parents, maintaining the connection to their parents is an important component of separation-individuation (Josselson, 1987). All these theories point out that attachment theory may not necessarily need to be positioned in opposition to separation-individuation. Rather, the two may be working together to have combined effects on students' adjustment to college.

Measured Effects of Attachment

More recent empirical literature on parent-student relationships at the college level focuses on attachment theory and its effects. A number of positive correlations have been found between students' having a secure base and experiencing success, particularly in the first year of college. Among the effects of attachment reflected in the literature are identity development, adjustment to college, academic success, and retention.

Identity Development

Evidence suggests that parent attachment in first-year college students is positively linked to identity development. For example, Samuolis, Layburn, and Schiaffino (2001) found that a female's identity development was related to her attachment to her parents. They did not draw the same conclusion for the male identity relationship, however, as identity was not significantly related to attachment with either parent. In addition, Samuolis, Layburn, and Schiaffino (2001) concluded that simply thinking about parents and being in frequent touch with them may be healthy and beneficial for identity development, particularly for female students. This conclusion departs from previous beliefs that high levels of attachment and contact lead to emotional distress. Lapsley, Rice, and Fitzgerald (1990) found that parental attachment predicted identity formation for both men and women.

Adjustment to College

Wintre and Yaffe (2000) studied how the discussion of university-related issues between students and parents affected the transition to college. They found that relationships with parents as well as discussion of issues directly affected adjustment. The implication of this conclusion is that students may benefit from the off-campus support of family as well as the support of on-campus resources during their first year.

Academic Success

Cutrona and others (1994) looked at attachment theory from the perspective of social support. They wanted to measure whether perceived social support from parents would influence academic performance in college during the first two years. They predicted that academic social support from family would cause students to have low anxiety and that low anxiety would in turn influence academic self-efficacy, or the belief that one has the ability to meet his or her goals. Academic self-efficacy would then be a predictor of the student's academic performance, which could be measured by his or her grade point average (GPA) (Cutrona and others, 1994). In fact, the study did show a positive correlation between parent support and GPA; parent support predicted higher GPAs across a heterogeneous sample group of varying majors and abilities (Cutrona and others, 1994).

Retention

These examples show that attachment has a mostly positive impact on college student development, specifically in the areas of identity development, adjustment to college, and academic success. But does a connection exist between the college student–parent relationship, attachment, and student retention? According to Tinto (1993), strong relationships with members of the community before coming to college facilitate adjustment and retention. Although the literature does not specifically explore the effects of parental attachment on retention at the higher education level, perhaps Tinto's theory could be applied to the student-parent relationship. This area needs more research.

Attachment and Residential Status

Some studies compare the effects of attachment by looking at residential and nonresidential populations of students. For example, Flanagan, Schulenberg, and Fuligni (1993) compared residential and nonresidential students, looking at ties to parents in both settings. The results showed that residential status had a significant effect on college students' perceptions of their relationships with their parents. Students living away from home reported more harmony in their relationship with parents, independence, and support, while students living at home reported more avoidant communication, rejection of parents as role models, and a greater tendency of parents to underestimate their sons and daughters' levels of maturity.

Berman and Sperling (1990) also examined the effects of residential status on relationships with parents and transition to college with somewhat different results. They reported stronger attachment relationships for commuter students. They found that parental attachment for residential students actually decreases over the first semester, while it remains unchanged for commuting students. According to the authors, this outcome may be attributed to the resident student's adjustment to the college environment and formation of new relationships that may take the place of the relationship with parents. In comparison, commuters who maintained a close physical proximity to their parents were found to maintain a higher level of attachment, which the authors say may be because they do not establish comparable peer friendships with those who are in residence (Berman and Sperling, 1990).

A New View of Student Development

Although administrators worry about the negative effects of parental involvement, we have shown through our review of the literature that parental involvement provides important benefits in terms of adjustment to college, academic success, and retention. How, then, can attachment theory as it relates to individuation help administrators and researchers to better understand the current levels of connection between college students and their parents? To understand today's college students, it may be necessary to think differently in terms of student development theory. Because the research shows strong student-parent relationships in college are beneficial, this theory might guide policy and action in dealing with students. We recommend practitioners use the lessons learned from attachment theory to reformulate how they think about student development and how these theoretical foundations shape their daily contact with both students and parents.

The use of attachment theory raised specific implications for college counselors and mental health centers. For example, Mattanah, Brand, and Hancock (2004) and Schwartz and Buboltz (2004) suggest college counselors consider students' level of attachment when evaluating them. Samuolis, Layburn, and Schiaffino (2001) say that if students show signs of homesickness, it could be directly related to their attachment to their parents. Students may miss home or their parents as a result of strong attachment relationships.

Another concept the literature discusses is that of parental involvement in campus life. Some studies point to positive effects from secure parent-student attachment, suggest involving parents in student life at college. For example, Hinderlie and Kenny (2002) recommend open communication with family members on the part of the college and suggest that colleges enable family members to play more of a role in campus life and feel more comfortable on campus. Wintre and Yaffe (2000) emphasize the importance of involving and educating parents about university life, because parents directly affect their students' adjustment to the university. Terenzini and others (1994) mention that it is important to orient parents as well as students so that they understand the nature of what students will be experiencing.

This research on attachment theory provides a challenge to Chickering's traditional model of separation-individuation (Chickering and Reisser, 1993). As it is one of the, if not the most, widely used theoretical bases in the field of student development and student affairs, this shift in thinking about relationships holds implications for student affairs professionals as well as faculty teaching student development (Taub, 1997). Graduate students in student affairs should be taught about the new models and how they may inform the old (Taub, 1997).

Students, Parents, and the Institution

T HE RELATIONSHIP BETWEEN COLLEGE STUDENTS and parents involves a key third player that cannot be ignored—the institution. Just as the relationship between parents and their students in college has changed over time, so too has the relationship between students and institutions and between parents and institutions. To consider these changes, we must examine the overarching question that guides discussion on this topic and provides perspective to the shifting relationship among these three parties: Are college students children or adults?

In Loco Parentis

In loco parentis is Latin for "in the place of a parent" (Gifis, 1996). In his 1770 description of English laws, William Blackstone applied this phrase to educators: "The father may also delegate part of his parental authority . . . to the tutor or schoolmaster of his child; who is then *in loco parentis,* and has such portion of the power of the parent committed to his charge, viz. that of restraint and correction as may be necessary to answer the purposes for which he is employed" (Zirkel and Reichner, 1987, p. 466). This doctrine of in loco parentis was later imported from English law as a protection for early American teachers who felt that it was necessary to administer corporal punishment to their pupils (Zirkel and Reichner, 1987). Over time, the doctrine of in loco parentis has been adapted to changes in both schools and society (Zirkel and Reichner, 1987).

History in Education

In the context of higher education, in loco parentis was a central tenet of the early colonial colleges. According to Henry Dunster, president of Harvard College from 1640–1644, the mission of the college of the seventeenth century was "to advance in all learning, divine and humane, each and every learned student who is or will be entrusted to your tutelage, according to their several abilities; and especially to take care that their conduct and their manners be honorable and without blame" (Thomas, 1991, p. 34). From the beginning, American higher education institutions closely monitored their students' behavior. The courts supported this stance in *Gott* v. *Berea College* in 1913. In *Gott,* several Berea College students were expelled after violating a college rule that they could not enter local establishments not controlled by the college. Gott, who owned a restaurant in the town, brought action against the college in an attempt to get it to do away with the rule. The court found in favor of the college, holding that the college may impose any rule or regulation "for the government or betterment of their pupils that a parent could do for the same purpose" (Thomas, 1991, p. 34).

In loco parentis was the predominant view of the relationship between the university and its students until the 1960s and 1970s, when, as a result of students' demands for more autonomy, a shift away from this model occurred and colleges began to take a more hands-off approach to students' conduct. The 1960s and 1970s were considered a period of turmoil, when college students continually challenged the administration's policies and practices regarding student rights through collective and individual efforts (Grossi and Edwards, 1997). At the same time that the traditional power structure of the university was crumbling, so too was the traditional power structure of the family. Increasingly parents lost their status as authority figures and control of their children in college (Brubacher and Rudy, 1997).

As a result of the shift in philosophy about the relationship between students and the university during this time, new policies were implemented to reflect students' increasing independence. The Family Educational Rights and Privacy Act (FERPA) was passed in 1974, placing restrictions on what information universities could share with parents. FERPA is also known as the Buckley amendment, as it was an amendment to the Educational Amendments of 1974 sponsored by Senator James Buckley (Lowery, 2005). It is a "spending clause statute," which means that it applies to any school that receives federal funds from a U.S. Department of Education program. FERPA grants three main rights to college students (or to parents if students are younger than 18): (1) the right to inspect and review or the right to access their education records; (2) the right to challenge the content of their education records; and (3) the right to consent to the disclosure of their education records (Family Educational Rights and Privacy Act, 20 U.S.C. §1232g [1974]). Once a student is older than 18 or enrolled in a higher education institution, the school must have written permission from the student to release any information from his or her educational record to any party. Certain people such as school officials with "legitimate educational interest" qualify as an exception to this rule, but parents of a student age 18 or older are not exempt from the restrictions (Family Educational Rights and Privacy Act, 20 U.S.C. §1232g [1974]).

FERPA formalized a hands-off approach for colleges and universities not only in terms of communication with families but also in terms of oversight of students. Regulations of visiting hours in residence halls, policies related to overnight guests of the opposite gender, and other policies related to personal lifestyle were relaxed. This hands-off approach was relatively short lived, however. Beginning in the 1980s, colleges gradually began a return to controlling, regulating, and disciplining their students (Weigel, 2004). Students began to expect more services from colleges such as career placement, tuition assistance, protection against criminal attack and harm inflicted by others, and safeguards against injuries that resulted from their own carelessness (Gibbs and Szablewicz, 1988). As a result, today's colleges offer a myriad of services and protections for their students, from stricter codes of student conduct to security doors on residence halls and attendants at the front desks of the halls to check in residents and their guests (Weigel, 2004).

Since the initial demise of in loco parentis, some have argued that it has returned, as students and parents as well as the courts are forcing institutions to take increasing responsibility for students' behavior. Although the relationship between the university and the student has evolved since the 1960s and 1970s, it is difficult to produce a clear definition today. A tension exists in the literature between whether in loco parentis may have returned (Gibbs and Szablewicz, 1988) or whether a new version of this relationship has emerged (Grossi and Edwards, 1997). What should the ideal relationship be between the university and the student?

Legal History

Lately neither universities nor students have been the primary actors defining their relationship. One of the strongest influences on this relationship and its new form has been the legal system. In many ways, the trend toward more control over students' behavior reflects a general shift in the courts toward increasing protection for students.

After the shift in the student-institution relationship in the 1960s and the demise of in loco parentis, the courts began to view the university primarily as a bystander, and the school's liability for students' actions was limited. Cases that reflect the trend in the courts during this time include *Bradshaw* v. *Rawlings* (1979), *Baldwin* v. *Zoradi* (1981), *Beach* v. *University of Utah* (1986), and *Rabel* v. *Illinois Wesleyan University* (1987). In each case, the courts looked at the university's responsibility in terms of "duty" or "no duty" (Bickel and Lake, 1999, p. 50). For example, in *Bradshaw* a student was injured in a car accident when coming home from an off-campus school-sponsored sophomore picnic. *Baldwin* involved a student who was hurt in a car accident after consuming alcohol in a college dormitory. In *Rabel* a male student was to abduct a female student and run with her over his shoulder as part of a fraternity initiation. As the male student grabbed the female student and attempted to follow instructions, he fell, crushing her skull in the fall and causing permanent head injuries. In *Beach* a student on a camping field trip in the mountains of Utah fell from a cliff and was eventually rendered a quadriplegic. In all these cases, the newly empowered students were beyond the control of the university (Bickel and Lake, 1999), and the university had "no duty" for the behavior of these students and their safety (Bickel and Lake, 1999, p. 57).

This period and the institution's role as "bystander" were short lived. In the 1980s, courts began to hold colleges liable for personal injuries to students that occurred in a variety of different contexts. In *Mullins* v. *Pine Manor College* (1983), an intruder came onto the Pine Manor College campus through an unlocked gate and raped a student. The court found that the college was responsible because of existing social norms and assumed duties. Once the institution assumes a particular duty, the courts say, the institution must fulfill it. For example in *Mullins*, Pine Manor assumed a duty of care by having security personnel who patrolled the campus. The college did not fulfill its duty, however, because no one checked to make sure the gate was locked. The holding stated that parents, students, and the general community have the expectation that reasonable care will be used to protect students from foreseeable harm.

Mullins was significant because it showed that the student-institution relationship is special (Gibbs and Szablewicz, 1988). Unlike a case just three years earlier, *Mullins* resulted in a ruling that did find the institution responsible for negligent behavior. In 1980 in *Relyea* v. *State of New York,* the plaintiff sought damages from her public college after she was attacked on the college grounds. The court held that a landowner has the duty to protect others on his or her property from criminal acts if such acts are foreseeable but that generally the landowner is not responsible for ensuring the safety of his or her invitees (Gibbs and Szablewicz, 1988).

Since the 1980s, colleges have increasingly been held responsible for unsafe acts that occur on their property, even acts of students. For example, the ruling in *Furek* v. *University of Delaware* led to increasing liability for student activity in fraternity houses on college property. In *Furek,* a student poured lye-based liquid oven cleaner on another student pledging a fraternity during "hell week." Although the university did not own the fraternity, the fraternity house was on university property. Consequently, the Delaware Supreme Court found that the university was liable. In this case, the court determined that the university had assumed a duty to protect its students from incidents of hazing. The school had warned students about the effects of hazing and had tried to discipline some students for it. Because the university knew that hazing occurred in fraternities, it could not abandon its duty of care to protect its students from these acts of harm. *Furek* also emphasized the university's responsibility to regulate and supervise foreseeable dangerous activities. Overall, in both *Mullins* and *Furek,* colleges were held liable, even when they might have tried to protect their students (White, 2005).

Many of the significant court cases involving increasing university responsibility for students' behavior and even much literature on the possible resurrection of in loco parentis (or the emergence of the new in loco parentis) concern the 1980s, when the trend for increasing responsibility for and therefore stricter control of students was just beginning. And the trend toward even more oversight of students' behavior, on and off campus, continues today. Colleges have seen an increasing number of lawsuits, specifically arising from students' deaths. For example, the parents of Scott Krueger, who died in 1997 from alcohol poisoning five weeks into his freshman year at the Massachusetts Institute of Technology, brought suit against the university for their son's death. Under campus housing policies at the time, first-year students had to decide whether to live in a dormitory or fraternity house, which was considered college-sponsored housing. Krueger chose to live in a fraternity house and then took part in the fraternity's pledge process. On Animal House Night, he and his fellow pledges were instructed to drink a prescribed amount of alcohol. Krueger ended up in a coma and later died (Reisberg, 2000). MIT eventually settled, acknowledging that it was partly responsible for Krueger's death and paying $6 million to the Krueger family (Reisberg, 2000). As a result of the Krueger case, MIT changed its housing policy, requiring students to live in residence halls during their first year.

Even more recently in summer 2007, two administrators, the dean of students and director of Greek life at Rider University in Lawrenceville, New Jersey, were charged with aggravated hazing when an eighteen-year-old student died of alcohol poisoning after a fraternity initiation activity (Waley, 2007). This case was particularly surprising to legal experts because the charges brought against the college officials were criminal ones. Civil cases typically have been the avenue for issues of negligence. Although the charges against the two administrators were eventually dropped, this case might represent an even further shift in the university's legal responsibility for its students. Higher education is situated in an increasingly litigious society where parents not only expect colleges to look after the safety of their students but sue them if they do not.

Even FERPA, the federal law that was the hallmark for ending in loco parentis, has changed to reflect the changing student-university relationship. Since its inception, FERPA has been amended to allow additional sharing of information, in particular with parents. First, an institution of higher education may release personally identifiable information from a student's educational record to parents without the student's consent if the student is considered a dependent on the parents' tax records. Institutions have taken advantage of this provision to facilitate communication with parents (Lowery, 2005). Although FERPA continues to put ownership of academic records in the hands of students, colleges and universities have responded to the perpetual question from parents, "I'm paying the bill, so why can't I *see* the bill?" Increasingly, colleges and universities are clarifying how parents can get access to students' records, explaining that students can grant access to them. With electronic records, that process has become simpler. Schools are now posting online procedures for students to grant that information to their parents, and parents can view the information on the Web when they have access to their student's password.

FERPA was also amended to allow but not require institutions to notify parents when students under the age of twenty-one have violated campus policies regarding the use of alcohol or other drugs. Institutions have taken varying stances on notifying parents. Some automatically send letters home as a result of a policy violation; others reserve the right to contact parents for more extreme circumstances. Still others have chosen not to notify parents about alcohol and drug violations.

Another significant policy change showing the shifting student-institution relationship and parents' role in shaping it is the Campus Security Act of 1990, or the Jeanne Clery Disclosure of Campus Security Policy and Campus Crime Statistics Act (20 U.S.C. §1092(f) [1990]). As a result of this act, which the parents of Jeanne Clery lobbied for after she was raped and murdered by another student at Lehigh University, institutions must prepare an annual security report for students and employees and provide a summary to prospective students and employees. Parents increasingly use this information to evaluate the schools their children are considering attending, as safety and security is one of their top concerns (Lowery, 2005; Warwick and Mansfield, 2003). In general, parents and the general public increasingly are holding colleges accountable for taking care of their students, who have not quite reached adult status.

One view of the current relationship between students and the institution can be defined as *consumerism,* as the student receives certain goods and services in exchange for tuition and fees, which is a contractual relationship (Fass,

Morrill, and Mount, 1986). Others say, however, that referring to the student-institution relationship in this way is problematic because the institution should not be seen as a babysitter or a bystander but as an educator and facilitator (Bickel and Lake, 1997). So what is the relationship between colleges and students today? What should the ideal relationship between the university and the student be?

We know it is one that is shifting, with increasing responsibility for the university and decreasing freedom for students. It is often defined by external forces such as the legal system as well as by parents themselves, who have their own ideas about the relationship between the institution and students. Some authors have suggested viewing the student-institution relationship as the result of the changing social climate on campus. One idea includes a model of shared community and joint decision making: because today's college students actually expect and want adults to exercise control over their college experiences, colleges need to find a way to respond to these desires (Fass, Morrill, and Mount, 1986). Hoekema (1994) suggests colleges take neither the restrictive stance of in loco parentis nor a permissive stance but act instead *in loco avunculi* (in place of the uncle) and influence behavior through pathways other than discipline. Similarly, Willimon and Naylor (1995) propose a model in which the institution adopts a doctrine of *in loco amicis,* where the university serves as a "wise friend" and promotes nurturing friendships with adults.

In an era where students and parents demand that colleges take increasing responsibility for students' well-being, what should the relationship between university and student be? What are administrators to do? If higher education institutions do not decide and explain the kind of relationships they expect with students and with parents, the danger exists that external forces will make those decisions for them.

College Students: Children or Adults?

The purported return of in loco parentis raises some significant questions for higher education and for society that also affect the definition of the relationship between college students and their parents. The dominant, overarching issue is whether traditional-age college students should be considered as children or adults. Although cultural shifts caused the demise of in loco parentis in higher education, one place where it remained intact was in K–12 schools (Zirkel and Reichner, 1987). But what makes a college student different from a high school student? Does a birthday or a high school diploma grant adult status? Are today's college students children or adults? Can they be either, neither, or both?

In some contexts, both the institution and society view the college student as a child (or adolescent) and in some as an adult. College students can have credit cards in their own name (with or without having an income), drive, and vote, and, according to FERPA, they own their academic records. At the same time, though, they cannot drink legally until age twenty-one, must report their parents' income on financial aid forms, and cannot rent a car until they are twenty-five. Overall, their status is unclear.

What Do Students Think?

How do today's college students answer this central question? Do traditional-age college students see themselves as children or adults? Very few studies ask students about this question. A study by Arnett (1994), however, surveyed college students about their conceptions of the transition to adulthood and their own status as adults. Only 23 percent of those studied indicated that they considered themselves to have reached adulthood (Arnett, 1994). College students were also asked what characteristics were necessary to reach adulthood. Most college students did not think it was necessary to have completed schooling to enter adulthood, and only 27 percent considered full-time employment necessary for adulthood (Arnett, 1994). Historically, getting married and having children have been seen as two of the most significant markers of adult status, but only 15 percent of the students Arnett studied said that marriage was necessary for a person to be considered an adult and only 12 percent considered it necessary to be a parent.

For the students in Arnett's study, the most significant criteria indicating the transition to adulthood were emotional markers. Relationship to parents played a strong role in the perception of their status as adults. Although only 14 percent considered it necessary for a person to be "not deeply tied to parents emotionally" to be considered an adult, 72 percent agreed that establishing a relationship with parents on an equal standing was a necessary component of adulthood (Arnett, 1994, p. 220). The results of Arnett's study indicate that not only is the definition of adulthood unclear to administrators and to parents but also to students themselves. As noted previously, only one-quarter of the students in Arnett's study said that they think they have reached adulthood, and nearly two-thirds responded that they thought they had reached adulthood in some respects but not others (Arnett, 1994).

A New Understanding?

The institutional view of students is that they are sometimes children—for example, when the institution stands in loco parentis and is held responsible for students' behavior—and sometimes adults—as when the institution protects students' records from parents and other outside parties under FERPA. Parents too seem to view their students as both children and adults. Even students are confused about which category they fall into. So, what does it mean?

For today's traditional-age college students, the dichotomy of child versus adult is problematic. Perhaps we should adopt a new way of viewing college students and their developmental stages that is more flexible. Arnett (2000a, 2006) suggests that college students have their own category—somewhere between child and adult. He calls this period "emerging adulthood" and proposes a theory to describe the developmental period from the late teens through the twenties, with a specific focus on ages eighteen through twenty-five. According to Arnett (2000a, 2006), "emerging adulthood" is neither adolescence nor young adulthood but theoretically and empirically distinct from both. It is defined by a relative independence from social roles and normative expectations (Arnett, 2000a, 2006). Its main features are exploration of identity, instability, a focus on self, and feeling "in between": According to Arnett, very few people beyond age eighteen see themselves as adolescents, but they do not see themselves as adults either. Arnett's theory applies to emerging adults of all backgrounds and social classes, although he says that emerging adults from lower socioeconomic statuses are distinctive in that they are even more likely than higher socioeconomic status emerging adults to believe that their lives will be better than their parents' lives (Arnett, 2000b).

Pavela (1992) also suggests creating a new developmental category for college students, although he does so in the context of the legal relationship between student and institution. According to Pavela (1992), the term "adolescents" does not quite apply to college students, yet the term "young adults" suggests a level of maturity that he does not believe college students possess. Instead, he calls college students between the ages of eighteen and twenty-one "postadolescent preadults," or PAPAs (Pavela, 1992).

From this analysis, we can see how college students may not clearly fit into the category of child or adult. And authors such as Arnett (2000a, 2000b) and Pavela (1992) suggest that they deserve their own classification so that we may better understand them and meet their needs. But do college students need to fit in a developmental category at all? Perhaps this is the problem. It might be more helpful to administrators if we construct college student development more fluidly and understand college students to be on a continuum somewhere between but also including childhood and maturity.

If we stop seeing college as a time when students make a sudden transition from children to adults and view this construct as a false dichotomy, perhaps we would be better able to understand the phenomenon of parental involvement. It too could be viewed more fluidly. Because even though administrators as well as parents expect their students to develop independence at some point, that attainment of autonomy is a process that takes time and usually includes not only steps forward but also back. Moreover, these students to some extent will always be the children of their parents, even when they have children of their own.

Student Identity: Gender, Race, and Class

THIS CHAPTER EXAMINES THE LITERATURE on the influence of what we call "student identity variables," the specific student characteristics of gender, race, and socioeconomic class, and the effect of these variables on the relationship between traditional-age college students and their parents. The discussion is divided into three distinct sections—gender, race, and socioeconomic class—although the literature contains many overlaps of the three main variables.

Gender

How can the relationship between female college students and their parents be described? Is this relationship somehow different from the one that college males have with their parents, and if so, how? What are the effects of this relationship? Have they changed over time? Of the student identity variables discussed in this chapter, gender is the one about which the most has been written.

The predominant theory that underlies much of the research on female student-parent relationships is the theory of attachment, introduced in "Theoretical Grounding." As mentioned earlier, the relationship between self and other differs along gender lines. Females tend to favor relationships where a process of attachment is involved, and males tend to favor relationships where a process of separation is involved (Gilligan, 1993). Attachment theory may therefore better describe female students' relationships with their parents.

Some theorists argue that the relational nature of the attachment model supports the idea that women are different from men in their attachment to their parents. For example, Allen and Stoltenberg (1995) suggest it may be more important for women to retain close ties with family during the college years than men, but the literature is split on this issue. Although much research supports this idea, other theorists have still drawn the conclusion that no significant gender differences exist in attachment relationships. Why does this contradiction exist? Perhaps the nature of attachment is difficult to measure, or the measures used do not capture the complexity of the phenomenon, which causes the discrepancy in results regarding gender and attachment to parents.

As noted earlier, Lapsley, Rice, and Fitzgerald (1990) found an absence of significant gender differences in attachment to parents in their study of adolescent attachment to parents and peers. In addition, a study by Mattanah, Brand, and Hancock (2004) showed that secure attachment was associated with adjustment for both men and women, which challenges the idea that men strive for separation from relationships, while women strive for separation in relationships.

The connection between parents and college students is most frequently defined in terms of attachment and separation-individuation. Other central themes define the relationship between female college students and their parents, however, including emotional support from parents and parental expectations. This relationship between parents and their daughters in college has had a number of positive effects on students measured in the research. These effects can be categorized broadly as adjustment to college, identity development, and vocational and life choices.

Adjustment to College

The largest body of literature reflects the effects of parental attachment on students' adjustment to college. Research supports the idea that women who have stronger attachment relationships with their parents are more likely to successfully adapt to the college environment. For example, Kenny and Donaldson (1991) studied a sample of first-year college students and found that in general women considered themselves more attached to their parents when compared with men. In addition, those women who reported higher levels of attachment also reported higher levels of social competence and psychological well-being (Kenny and Donaldson, 1991). In Rice, Cunningham, and

Young's study of attachment to parents in both black and white college students (1997), women's attachment to both mother and father was significant in predicting social competence (attachment to mother alone was not a significant predictor). For the men in the sample, attachment to father was a more important predictor of social competence than attachment to mother.

Communication also plays a role in attachment to parents and adjustment to college. Sorokou and Weissbrod (2005) studied need- and non-need-based contact patterns between adolescents and their parents during the first year of college. Females initiated more non-need-based contact than the males in the study, but no differences occurred in initiation of need-based contact. In terms of attachment, females tended to perceive a higher-quality attachment to their mother, while males and females did not differ in their attachment to their father. A positive relationship existed between perceived quality of attachment and frequency of students' need- and non-need-based contact. In terms of receiving contact from parents, females received more need-based contact than males from both their mother and father. This observation shows that female students may differ in not only their perceived attachment relationships but also their contact patterns.

For women, positive adjustment has also been associated with a high degree of attitudinal dependence; women report holding beliefs and values similar to those of their parents. Schultheiss and Blustein (1994) note that separation-individuation actually may best be obtained through the context of adolescent-parent connectedness. In other words, students who are securely attached to their parents may have an easier time negotiating the process of individuation and adjusting to the new college environment.

In their study, Schultheiss and Blustein (1994) tested whether attitudinal independence and parental attachment were positively associated with adjustment and development of college students. Contrary to the researchers' expectations and the literature, their hypothesis was supported only partially—for the women but not for the men. The results suggest that women who share similar beliefs and attitudes as their parents and are strongly emotionally attached to both parents are likely to have developed autonomy. For men, neither psychological separation nor parental attachment was related to development. In terms of adjustment, no support was found for the effects of either psychological separation or parental attachment for women, and support was very limited for men. According to the authors, one implication of the results is that women who have access to emotional and intellectual relationships with their parents may be further developed than students who lack this access.

Development of Identity

Another effect of parental attachment relationships reflected in the literature is formation of identity. According to Samuolis, Layburn, and Schiaffino (2001), attachment to caregivers had more positive influence on the formation of identity than separation from them. Additional theoretical grounding for their study includes research on gender differences in parent-adolescent attachment relationships suggesting that women are more affected by attachment relationships than men. The study included both male and female first-year students. Results showed that for women, but not for men, attachment to mother and to father were both associated with positive identity development.

Taub (1997) examined autonomy and parental attachment in traditional-age undergraduate women. The primary research questions of whether autonomy and parental attachment vary by class year were based on Chickering's model of identity development. Taub also considered the question of whether parental attachment varied by race and ethnicity. Results included the observation that students did indeed display increased autonomy with class year (seniors were found to be significantly more autonomous than both first-year students and juniors). At the same time, however, parental attachment did not decrease significantly with the increase in autonomy: students could maintain contact with their families and still gain autonomy. In addition, women in the study gained significant emotional independence from their peers but did not make significant gains in emotional independence from parents.

According to Taub (1997), these findings support the idea that identity development for women may be a different process from the one Chickering described. Undergraduate women may actually become more autonomous without experiencing a break in parental attachment (Taub, 1997). In terms of her findings with regard to racial and ethnic differences, Taub (1997) found that Latinas in particular scored significantly higher than Asian women in the parental role of providing emotional support. Taub (1997) suggests that these findings reflect cultural differences in the relationships between these parents and their daughters in college. For example, Asian cultures usually stress a child's devotion to her family as well as place a value on emotional restraint (Taub, 1997). In Latino families, family unity and loyalty are stressed as well as cooperation among family members (Taub, 1997).

Although students' responses to leaving home have been well documented, parents' responses to a child's leaving home have not been routinely incorporated into studies of parent-student relationships (Bartle-Haring, Brucker, and Hock, 2002). Bartle-Haring, Brucker, and Hock's longitudinal study of first-year college students and seniors (2002), however, looked at how parents' perspective played a role in this transition. They examined the role of parental separation anxiety and adolescent identity development and found that when mothers feel comfortable providing a secure base for their children, their daughters' (and also sons') ability to explore their identities is greater. A mother's anxiety about her daughter's distancing does not seem to negatively affect the daughter's identity development. On the other hand, for fathers anxiety about their daughters' distancing does seem to affect the daughter's identity development. A daughter tends to interpret her father's anxiety as more connectedness, which has a negative effect on her identity development, detracting from her ability to explore and make commitments to identity issues on her own (Bartle-Haring, Brucker, and Hock, 2002).

Surrey (1991) proposed a theory of women's identity development very similar to attachment theory called "self in relation." Her theory differs from traditional developmental theory, which emphasizes the importance of separation, because the construction of self for women may not be explained by this model (Surrey, 1991). According to Surrey, the primary experience for women is relational, and their sense of self is organized and developed in the context of important relationships. Surrey (1991) claims that the mother-daughter relationship is the "purest example" of this theory (p. 54). As the early mother-daughter relationship grows over the life cycle, it serves as a precursor to how women will learn, experience pleasure, and enhance themselves through relatedness (Surrey, 1991).

Vocational and Life Choices

Another body of literature measures the effect of parental relationships—and more specifically parental expectations—on females' vocational and life choices. Research shows that attachment may actually play a positive role in career exploration. For example, Ketterson and Blustein (1997) considered gender by comparing the overall levels of exploratory activity, defined as exploration of one's personal values and interests as well as relevant educational and career environments. The authors also looked at traditional career choices of men and women. Their study was grounded in the concepts that adolescent-parent relationships are important in the process of seeking a career and that secure attachment relationships between college students and their parents can lead to more exploration. Without broad searching, the authors suggested, college students, women in particular, are less likely to choose a career that is not based on gender stereotypes and uses their full array of talents. The results of their study showed that age, attachment to mother, and attachment to father were associated with more self- and environmental exploration.

Parental expectations and support can also play a role in female students' choice of career. In particular, it has been found to be true for women pursuing careers in science. For example, the objective of Rayman and Brett's study (1995) addressing the underrepresentation of women in scientific fields was to examine factors associated with persistence in the sciences for young women who majored in science and mathematics as undergraduates at a top women's college. Among other conclusions regarding the various independent variables, the researchers found that a mother's or a father's encouragement to pursue a career in science contributed significantly to the subject's choosing to stay in science after graduation. Support from both parents was even more significant than an individual parent's support. Rayman and Brett also considered whether one or two parents were in science themselves, but this factor did not seem to contribute significantly to whether a student stayed in a science field. Moreover, an interaction occurred between the variables of encouragement from parents and career advice from faculty.

Does a gender-related connection exist between frequency of communication and transmission of parental expectations? Smith and Self (1980) argue

that such a connection exists. Although their study may be a bit dated, they found that mothers' attitudes were important predictors of daughters' attitudes and that college-educated mothers showed more similar attitudes with their daughters than mothers who did not go to college. A main explanation for this observed phenomenon was that by interacting more frequently with their daughters, mothers simply may have a greater opportunity to share their views and attitudes with their daughters.

Implications

College administrators, in particular mental health counselors, and perhaps career advisors should consider college women differently from men in terms of their relationship with parents, acknowledging that female students may be affected differently by interactions with parents. Women may need to retain close ties while in school more than men do because of female students' relational nature (Allen and Stoltenberg, 1995). Administrators should also recognize that attachment to parents does not necessarily indicate a lack of autonomy on the part of the student (Taub, 1997).

College administrators should also consider the importance of communication with parents, especially for female students. What is the student walking across the quad on her way to class with cell phone to her ear talking about with her mother? Although administrators may make judgments about students who call home "just to talk," the content of the conversation may not actually be significant. This non-need-based contact and checking in (Sorokou and Weissbrod, 2005) help to provide the female student with a secure base from which to explore.

Race

Although race may overlap with certain other identity variables discussed in this chapter, literature on the topic of the role of race in parent-college student relationships is relatively lacking. Theorists themselves acknowledge that this topic is underresearched and its absence noticeable. According to Mattanah, Brand, and Hancock (2004), more attention is needed to examine attachment, separation-individuation, and college adjustment across different racial and ethnic groups, because certain cultures, especially Asian, African, and Latino, emphasize collectivism and interdependence.

Some limited quantitative research has been undertaken in the area of attachment, however. For example, Hinderlie and Kenny (2002) studied attachment, social support, and college adjustment among black students at predominantly white universities. The authors acknowledged that black students have been found to value family ties but wondered whether a close family culture might impede adjustment to college. Their goal in the study was to explain more about the relationship between these students and their parents. Students in the sample were from six predominantly white and academically competitive institutions and represented a range of socioeconomic classes. Results of the study showed that parental attachment was positively associated with all aspects of college adjustment for these students. Relationships on campus with both peers and faculty were also key to black students' adjustment to college at these institutions. A combination of all these variables therefore creates the best formula for students' adjustment to college, emotional stability, and academic success (Hinderlie and Kenny, 2002). In addition, Rice, Cunningham, and Young (1997) and Mounts (2004) compared parental attachment with black and white college students. Neither found significant differences in attachment bonds between these two populations.

In terms of qualitative research, Sanchez, Reyes, and Singh (2005) looked at the role of significant relationships in the academic experiences of a sample they describe as Mexican American college students. They found that students reported their parents provided different types of support: cognitive guidance, emotional support, informational and experiential support, modeling, and tangible support (Sanchez, Reyes, and Singh, 2005). These types of support are not that far from attachment. The love of parents in combination with practical support from educational sources, especially in the area of scholarships and financial aid, is what made them successful.

Barnett (2004) looked at the ways in which family support contributed to persistence and graduation for black students at an Ivy League university and to what extent family support was essential for students' success and adaptation to university life. From fifty interviews, the author found that family

support and interaction correlated with both social adjustment and institutional attachment. In this study black parents not only saw their students as having the potential to go to college and encouraged them to attend but also prepared their students for a "racist environment that depreciates African-American values, culture, and people" (Barnett, 2004, p. 54). Parents provided emotional support for their students, and they were able to communicate how proud they were of their children's accomplishments as well as how to navigate the stresses of a predominantly white university (Barnett, 2004). According to one student, his mother was his primary source of emotional support. "Yeah, I call her for emotional support if I'm really having it bad or whatever I'll call her and I talk to her. Usually she's the one who is able to bring anything out of me to get me to talk about it or whatever. I may not want to talk about it with my friends or whatever and stuff, but she's like the person who can get me to just spill my guts out. She knows everything I've been through. Every single trial, tribulation, she knows what I've been through" (Barnett, 2004, p. 62). According to Barnett, 70 percent of males and 80 percent of females in the study reported that it was their parents' support and encouragement that helped them persist in college.

It is important to note when considering the experiences of the students in Barnett's study that 84 percent of the students' parents had attended some college, 38 percent of the students came from homes where both parents had gone to college, and 14 percent of the students' parents had some sort of post-baccalaureate education. These parents' experiences with higher education may play a role in the type of support they are able to provide to their students (Barnett, 2004, p. 63). Parents' educational level may also have influenced the analysis, as these parents may have been well positioned to offer advice to their students about college life. This study also shows, however, the importance of an attachment relationship and a secure base for the black students the researcher studied. Barnett acknowledges that family interactions of black students have been largely ignored in the literature.

Mallinckrodt (1988) also studied the experience of black students. Specifically, his study looked at the relationship between persistence and perceptions of social support from members of the campus community as well as family members (Mallinckrodt, 1988). He found that perceived encouragement from family members correlated to persistence for white students but not for black students. The factor that was most strongly associated with persistence for black students in the study was a relationship with someone in the campus community, measured by the extent to which students in the study agreed with the statement, "I am pretty satisfied with the quality of the close relationships I have with people here at school" (Mallinckrodt, 1988, p. 62). These results seem to conflict with those found by Barnett (2004). Although Mallinckrodt does not mention parents' education level as a variable in his study, perhaps educational background leads to the difference in perceptions of parental support for the students in the two studies.

Increasingly, student affairs personnel and academic leaders recognize the effects of multiple identities in an individual. Race and relationships with parents are primarily considered in literature when they are combined with other factors such as parents' level of education, socioeconomic status, and gender. The next section looks specifically at the student identity variable of socioeconomic class, including a discussion of the literature that describes the experiences of first-generation college students.

Culture may also play a role in the relationship between students of color and their parents. For example, Latinos are known to be very family oriented and consider their primary commitment to be to a group rather than to an individual (Padilla, Trevino, Gonzalez, and Trevino, 1997). This outlook may impact Latino students' decision to live away from home or the role of parents in their day-to-day lives (Terry, Dukes, Valdez and Wilson, 2005). Native Americans also tend to be very family oriented (Terry, Dukes, Valdez and Wilson, 2005). Asian students are significantly influenced by their parents, as this community often views academic success and achievement as important values. In addition, parental expectations may shape these students' choice of major (Terry, Dukes, Valdez and Wilson, 2005).

Some broad generalizations do not apply to every member of these groups, and although administrators should recognize that cultural background may play a role in the student-parent relationship, they should not assume anything about the relationship between any specific parent-student pair. Administrators should be aware of the role that culture plays between international college students and their parents, especially because these families are often located physically far away from their students and face barriers such as different languages and time zones.

Socioeconomic Class

Some K–12 literature shows that parents' participation or involvement in schooling varies by social class. For example, Lareau (1987) noted that the relationship between parental involvement and socioeconomic class was evident early in a child's education. For her study of differences in social class in family-school relationships, she acted as a participant-observer in two different first-grade classrooms in two different communities, one that she considered to be "working class" and one that she labeled "middle class."

According to Lareau (1987), the amount and quality of interaction differed between parents and their respective schools. Parents at the middle-class school were more involved. They responded more often to teachers' requests for involvement and had higher amounts of interaction at higher levels of quality than the parents at the other school. In some cases, teachers at the middle-class school reported examples of times when parental involvement was unhelpful (in particular, when parents challenged teachers' expertise [Lareau, 1987]). According to Lareau, much of this behavior seemed to be based on the more flexible schedule of the middle class, allowing more time for school contact and interaction with teachers. In addition, middle-class parents had social networks where they could learn about opportunities for involvement that working-class parents did not have access to. Lareau also concluded that institutions tended to promote the type of behavior exhibited by the middle-class parents.

Can Lareau's conclusion be applied to higher education? Does a link exist between socioeconomic class and parental involvement in college? Although this question is relatively unknown and unmeasured, a fair amount of literature is available on social class and the parent-student relationship during pre-college preparation. For both populations literature exists that describes the role parents can play in their children's preparation for college. This section looks to the literature on the parent-student relationship regarding preparation for college for lower and higher socioeconomic classes. This analysis provides important contextual information about how these different families approach higher education.

First-Generation College Students

In the discussion of students from lower socioeconomic status groups, it is important to include information about parents' education level and literature about first-generation college students, or students whose parents have no college or university experience (Billson and Terry, 1982; Pascarella, Pierson, Wolniak, and Terenzini, 2004; York-Anderson and Bowman, 1991). These two variables—parents' education level and socioeconomic status—are closely related because the definition of socioeconomic class status that we use for this analysis is not necessarily how much income one has but how much cultural capital one has, or the degree of ease one has with the dominant culture of society (Bourdieu, 1984). Parents' education level combined with parents' income is the best indicator of socioeconomic status (Astin and Oseguera, 2004).

It is particularly important to look at this group of students because it seems that parental involvement and students' perceptions of this parental involvement differ. For example, although most students perceived amounts of parental involvement in their lives as being "just right," first-generation students, and Latino students in particular, were more likely to say that their parents had "too little" involvement, particularly with regard to choosing college activities and courses but also in terms of helping with college applications and influencing college choice (Higher Education Research Institute, 2008).

Research has shown that first-generation college students tend to be at a disadvantage when it comes to having basic knowledge about postsecondary education as a result of their lack of cultural capital (Pascarella, Pierson, Wolniak, and Terenzini, 2004). Individuals with highly educated parents may have an advantage over these students in understanding the culture of higher education (Pascarella, Pierson, Wolniak, and Terenzini, 2004). As we will see through the next section, parents of higher-socioeconomic status groups play a strong role in "managing" their children's pathways to college (Auerbach, 2004, p. 126; McDonough, 1997). Parents of students in lower-socioeconomic groups may offer support for their children's desire to attend college, but few of these families without a tradition of attending college themselves have enough knowledge to be able to help their children navigate the pathways to college (Auerbach, 2004, p. 126). In general, first-generation students and their parents tend to have less congruity between students' and their parents' values toward education, and they receive less overall support from their parents toward their educational goals, both financial and emotional (Billson and Terry, 1982). Levels of parental involvement in the college admissions process have been found to be lower for students from lower-socioeconomic families than they are for students from higher-socioeconomic families (Cabrera and La Nasa, 2000, 2001).

One area of literature about first-generation college students from low-income backgrounds that is applicable to this topic is the literature on college preparation programs. These programs, many of which include a parental education component, help first-generation students and parents gain some of the cultural capital they lack. A main function of these programs is to increase college awareness for parents so that their expectations for their children's education are increased (Perna, 2002). College preparation programs can be defined as outreach activities designed to identify and assist underrepresented students on their paths to college. These programs are primarily funded through the efforts of educational institutions, state and federal governments, and local communities (Tierney, Corwin, and Colyar, 2005).

A survey of fifty college access and parental involvement programs in California found that these programs were the main source of college information for program participants (McDonough and others, 2000). Examples of how these programs, specifically the federally funded TRIO programs, provide this information to parents include parent orientation programs; frequent phone calls to discuss their children's progress in the program; parent-student advising sessions; invitations to parents to participate in field trips and program activities; parent advisory boards, newsletters, handbooks, and workshops; and invitations to families to attend graduation ceremonies and student presentations or exhibitions (Becker, 1999; Zulli, Frierson, and Clayton, 1998). Despite these many initiatives, however, a study of precollege outreach programs targeting low-income students, historically underrepresented minorities, and first-generation students found that one of the biggest challenges was coordination with parents. Tierney (2002) also notes that a discrepancy still exists between the research showing that parental involvement in precollege preparation programs is good and the actual practice of family involvement in precollege outreach programs. More of these efforts are needed.

Ceja's qualitative study (2006) focused on parents and their role in the transition to college. The participants in Ceja's series of three interviews were first-generation college-bound Chicanas from low-socioeconomic backgrounds. Although the parents wanted the best for their students, they did not have the same notion of college "fit" as parents of higher-socioeconomic groups, because these parents did not attend college. Through his constant-comparative analysis of interviews, Ceja (2006) found that the role parents were able to fulfill during the college choice process was actually greatly limited. The parents lacked a formal understanding of the college choice process. This lack of familiarity was true for all the Chicanas in the study, regardless of their level of academic achievement (Ceja, 2006). For example, one student in the study described feeling that the college choice process was entirely up to her. "I've told them the schools and I am going to [apply] and they ask me, 'Where is that at?' and 'Why do you want to go there?' I tell them that it is a good school. It's like they don't know anything about it and they [can't] help me out with the college choice process. I think that's all been left to me" (Ceja, 2006, p. 95). As a result of their parents' lack of information about colleges and the college choice process, students in the study found that they were engaged in the double-duty task of learning and experiencing the college choice process themselves while also informing and familiarizing their parents with it (Ceja, 2006, p. 98).

Smith (2001) also found that parents who did not attend college lacked clarity about the college choice process. In an ethnographic study at a high school in South Central Los Angeles, Smith looked at the college choice process for low-socioeconomic black students, interviewing both parents and students. He concluded ultimately that the parents of the students in his study had what he termed "soft knowledge," or a fuzziness of knowledge about college applications, finances, and admission procedures and college life (Smith, 2001, p. 18). According to Smith, this soft knowledge is most visible in discussions about the SATs; for example, one parent expressed her confusion when she said, "But he's still taking the SAT test to bring his average up higher, you know, so he can have a high SAT. . . . One of the [coaches from the] schools that wants him to come play for them tried to explain a little bit of it to me too about the SATs" (Smith, 2001, p. 18). In this particular case, the student had to explain to his mother what the SAT is for and why it is important. Like the students in Ceja's study, the student in this particular example takes on the role of trying to educate his mother about the college process while trying to navigate it himself. Such input is not very useful to students in the college choice process (Smith, 2001).

If a student's parents attended college, the experience is significantly different from that of first-generation students. Karp, Holmstrom, and Gray (2004) interviewed thirty sets of upper-middle-class parents for a grounded-theory study of the ways college-educated parents evaluate the meaning of their children's leaving home to attend college. The authors observed that the parents in their study expressed many worries about their students' transition to college but that these fears were different from those expressed by parents of first-generation college students. In particular, a central concern of parents was whether their children had chosen the right college. Parents seemed to have the idea that the fit at some colleges on their students' lists of potential choices might be better than at others (Karp, Holmstrom, and Gray, 2004, p. 367). According to the researchers' analysis, these parental worries were often rooted in parents' own experiences of leaving home to attend college. In one interview a parent stated, "Yeah, I think it's very important to find a place that's a good match, that's, you know, a match for his ability and it's an environment that will be supportive of him. I had a rough time my first semester in college" (Karp, Holmstrom, and Gray, 2004, p. 367). Parents who did not attend college may not express the same fears, especially about the idea of college fit.

Parental involvement and encouragement are important to all students in their college choice process, but they are particularly important to students from low socioeconomic classes because such students are less likely to consider college as an option early in their schooling and are also less likely to persist if they do enroll (Stage and Hossler, 2000). Parental support and encouragement are the best predictors of postsecondary educational aspirations (Stage and Hossler, 1989; Hossler, Schmidt, and Vesper, 1999). Parental encouragement can be defined by the frequency of parents' and students' discussions about parents' expectations, hopes, and dreams for their children with regard to attending college. Parental support is more tangible and includes behaviors such as parents' saving money for college, visiting college campuses, and attending financial aid workshops (Hossler, Schmidt, and Vesper, 1999). Parental support and encouragement play a much more significant role in shaping educational aspirations of their children than either their educational background or income level (Hossler, Schmidt, and Vesper, 1999).

Students' Experience of Parents' Role in the Transition to College

What is students' experience of parental involvement in the transition to college? How do students in these studies view their relationship with their parents? What role do parents play in the college admission and adjustment process, according to these students? Some students view their parents as playing strong roles, setting the expectation that students will even pursue higher education. For example, Attinasi (1989) conducted an exploratory study from Mexican American students' point of view regarding the context surrounding their decisions to persist or not persist in higher education. Through his interviews of eighteen students, he found that oral communication of expectations was extremely important to students. Parents played an important role in that they communicated to their children the fact that they belonged in the category of college-goers (Attinasi, 1989). A student's willingness to "stick it out" once in college seemed to reflect preparation for college from parents (Attinasi, 1989, p. 270).

Some students reported experiencing anxiety over a changing relationship with parents and other family members. Students in Terenzini and others' focus groups (1994) for a study on the transition to college, particularly those from black, Hispanic, or Native American families, reported that as parents (or other parental figures such as grandparents) realize that their students might never metaphorically "return home," they have tried to maintain a consistent relationship that the students realize may be changing (Terenzini and others, 1994, p. 66). One student described this tension: "My grandmother. Even though she is a big inspiration to me, uh, she has this way of clinging. She hates to let go of things. And I can understand. I think that's why she takes in a lot of us, as we're going along. She hates to let us go" (Terenzini and others, 1994, p. 66).

In the transition to college, students' development of independence and their own identity formation is influenced by these relationships with parents. Torres (2004) looked at familial influences on the identity development of Latino first-year students through a longitudinal study of first-year students and a grounded-theory analysis. She found that family members were the primary conveyors of cultural heritage for students and that the development of students' ethnic identity was determined by the degree to which parents were acculturated or the degree to which they intermingled Latino and Anglo cultures (Torres, 2004).

According to London (1989), one of the biggest challenges for first-generation students is reconciling the tension that emerges between requirements of family membership and upward mobility. For many first-generation students, a personal growth from their student experience may be accompanied by a loss in their relationship with their family (London, 1989). Some parents give students conflicting messages: to stay at home and to achieve in the outside world, which causes an internal struggle for this population (London, 1989). Students speak of this push-pull and their struggle to find their own voices amid the echo from home (London, 1989). As one student in London's study mentioned about her experience with her mother, "She has this idea that I'm way up there somewhere and she wants to drag me back" (p. 160). Because of this tension, first-generation college students may internalize feelings of shame rather than taking pride in their upward mobility (Duffy, 2007).

When students move into this "other" culture, they may have to renegotiate relationships with their families as well as with themselves (London, 1992, p. 6). These students find themselves living on the "margins of two cultures" (London, 1992, p. 7). One student in London's study said she felt she was "living in both worlds" (p. 8). The very act of going to college may signify to the family that the student is interested in moving into the middle class and attaining a white-collar position not previously held by a member of the family (London, 1992). Even if students are not necessarily concerned with upward mobility, they still may struggle when they find themselves in a new social status group at college. Sometimes they test the reactions of their family members by "trying on" and experimenting through displaying cultural symbols and artifacts of this higher social group (London, 1992, p. 7). This experimentation may cause concern for family members about the student's outward changes.

Rendon (1992), an education professor and scholar, describes the "pain of separation" (p. 58) she personally experienced as a poor, first-generation college student in her essay "From the Barrio to the Academy: Revelations of a Mexican American 'Scholarship Girl.'" She talks about the fear that both she and her mother experienced during this transition. When Rendon asked her mother why she was afraid of Rendon's leaving home to be on her own, to be by herself, her mother told her, "I am afraid—I don't know why" (p. 59). Rendon too was scared. "I sensed that deep in my mother's soul she felt resentful about how this alien culture of higher education was polluting my values and customs. I, in turn, was afraid that I was becoming a stranger to her, a stranger she did not quite understand, a stranger she might not even like" (p. 59).

Parental Experiences of Students' Transition to College

What about parents' perspective of their children's transition to college? How does the literature reflect this experience? This viewpoint too may be influenced by where students attend college and whether parents perceive that students are "leaving home" or not. This expectation may also be based on socioeconomic class. The parents in Karp, Holmstrom, and Gray's study (2004) experienced this phenomenon as their students prepared to attend residential four-year institutions. "Separation and individuation are issues that must be faced by all human beings, but leaving home in its American sense is not [universal]. Especially for upper-middle class families, leaving home for a residential college is a major rite of passage for both children and their parents" (Karp, Holmstrom, and Gray, 2004, p. 358). Therefore, according to this analysis, even if some students do not permanently move out of their parents' residences when they attend school, parents may view them as symbolically "leaving home" because of the individuation traditionally associated with the act of attending college.

It seems that all parents experience at least some anxiety about their children's leaving home, regardless of socioeconomic class and their own educational level. Most parents also share the value of wanting students to seek higher education, even if parents lack knowledge about the college admissions process. Ceja (2006) concludes that a lack of parental understanding of the college process should not be confused with a lack of support or encouragement. One student in Ceja's study noted that her mother did not understand her approach of applying to many different schools to expand her choices. Nonetheless, her mother was supportive of her daughter's decision to attend college. The student noted that "all she tells us is just to pick a good school somewhere, [to] pick the best one" (Ceja, 2006, p. 94).

Karp, Holmstrom, and Gray (2004) point out that "empty nest syndrome" is largely class based, as different meanings are associated with a child's leaving home. Even though parents in Karp, Holmstrom, and Gray's study (2004) did report anxiety about the transition to college, these parents largely defined this empty nest period as positive, perhaps the result of different expectations for independence and attachment or perhaps because upper-middle-class parents with greater resources might have greater life options than less affluent parents whose children no longer live at home (Karp et al., 2004).

Another potentially class-based parent experience that emerges from the literature is parents' reaction to college officials and administrators in the college choice and transition process. According to Smith (2001), in a study of Black students at a low socioeconomic high school, as a result of the lack of clarity that parents experience in the college admissions process, parents perceived college staff as a malevolent "collective they" (p. 18).

Upper-Middle-Class Parents and the College Admissions Process

In considering the parent-student relationship and college access, we also need to look at upper-middle-class students and their approach to the college admissions process, particularly at highly selective institutions. These students have involved parents who want their children to attend the "best college" and who often serve as the source of pressure for students in the admissions process because of their desire for a return on their investment, both the future investment of tuition dollars and the past financial cost of raising a child (Karen, 2002; Mathews, 1998; McDonough, 1997; Robbins, 2006). Their parents have been highly involved at every stage of the game, providing them with the best opportunities to set them up for this moment in time, including a number of services for hire from the "right" kindergarten to private college counselors and SAT review courses (Karabel, 2005; Lareau, 1987).

Upper-middle-class parents typically see their child's attendance at a residential college as necessary for perpetuating their class position. In fact, upper-middle-class family life is often organized around the singular pursuit of a child's education (Holmstrom, Karp, and Gray, 2002; Karen, 2002; McDonough, 1997). This section examines the college admissions process from the point of view of upper-middle-class students and their families who are applying to selective institutions, considering the intense competition for places in the freshman classes of elite colleges and universities by those who have the economic capital to attend them.

Higher Education as a Consumer Good

Who are upper-middle-class students (also called "privileged" and "the dominant class")? What characterizes this group? Labeled "overachievers" by Alexandra Robbins and "organization kids" by David Brooks, the generation of upper-middle-class students seeking entrance to the nation's selective colleges and universities are busy. They work hard and live structured lives that encompass myriad activities from athletics to clubs to volunteering, all of which will eventually be marketed in trying to attain admission to the elusive "best college" (Fitzsimmons, McGrath, and Ducey, 2006). For the most part, they attend elite public and private high schools, often viewed as having one function—to get them into the "best" colleges (Karen, 2002; Mathews, 1998).

In searching, most students seek schools they perceive to be appropriate or schools where they will feel comfortable (McDonough, 1997). For some students, the "best" college is one that has prestige and name recognition, often referred to as a "brand-name school." In *The Overachievers: The Secret Life of Driven Kids,* journalist Robbins chronicles the experiences of teens at Walt Whitman High School, a public high school in an upper-middle-class suburb of Washington, D.C., which she describes as "not an underprivileged school" (2006, p. 16). Of the students she followed, most were fortunate enough to choose among colleges without regard for tuition costs (p. 16). One student described one characteristic of the best college for him. "I like the idea of having a school with a name that's respected. It's a really attractive idea because of the push to go to a school that people have heard of for the prestige" (Robbins, 2006, p. 186).

According to Riesman (1980), the quest for the best college has some origins in Jewish students' trying to gain admission to college during the post–World War II era. Although a small and marginalized group, they wanted for themselves and their families wanted for them whatever college was defined in the national system of prestige as being "the best." Riesman himself, however, calls this viewpoint absurd and points out that as consumers, students should be concerned not with which is the best college but which is the *right* one for them.

> *Consumers Union in its Guides and Reports will rarely state that a particular car, for example, is "the best" for all purposes and situations; it may list a number of cars as among the best, noting various tradeoffs that the purchaser should take into account. The idea of assuming that there is an all-purpose "best" college is like assuming that athletic contests, in which it is possible to say who can run a particular distance the fastest . . . who can pole vault the highest, and so on, could set a national trend that one can discover in every field a perennial "best" [Riesman, 1980, p. 54].*

A ranking system that attempts to label a college as "best" would not be possible, as individual choice must be involved in the process.

But pressure and competition are increasing to get into the best college. The competition is a process that has evolved over time. In the early part of the twentieth century, colleges like Harvard, Yale, and Princeton, which are now considered the colleges most selective and difficult to get into in the United States, had rather low admissions standards (Karabel, 2005). One did not need to be particularly academically accomplished to gain a place in the class at one of these schools; the main requirement was that one be "rich and socially inclined" (Karabel, 2005, p. 23). In fact, the Big Three waived admissions requirements for many of those students who were "paying customers" because of the schools' desire for tuition revenue. In 1907, for example,

55 percent of those admitted to Harvard had failed to fulfill the entrance requirements (Karabel, 2005, p. 22). As the rates of high school graduates increased and colleges such as those in the Ivy League started to recruit nationally, admissions standards began to tighten, and acceptance rates dropped (Riesman, 1980).

Over time, the definition of "merit" has also shifted in response to the transfer of power between different groups as well as changes in the broader society. The definition of merit is fluid and tends to reflect the values of those in positions of prestige who have the ability to impose their cultural ideals (Karabel, 2005, p. 3). Despite changes in the way merit is understood and the increase in access provided to previously underrepresented groups (such as women, historically underrepresented minorities, Jews, and groups from lower socioeconomic classes), those whom it predominantly serves are the privileged. Paying customers still constitute the majority of students at elite institutions (Karabel, 2005, p. 537). Bourdieu and Passeron's theory (1990) that social origin determines education and that education privileges the dominant classes is still largely visible in American higher education. Moreover, this feature of the system does not alleviate anxiety about who can get in. Even though paying customers largely benefit, it is not guaranteed that one will have access to the product he or she is hoping to obtain (McDonough, 1997). The uncertainty of the college admissions process is a large source of stress for the privileged classes. They can no longer be confident that they can pass their social position on to the next generation (Karabel, 2005). At the same time, students from less-privileged classes are about just as likely to attend institutions of higher education as they were in 1954 (Karabel, 2005).

Among those choosing college (even among the consumers paying full price), not everyone chooses a college with selective admissions standards. Only a small group of institutions are considered to have selective admissions coupled with a strong academic program (Riesman, 1980). Only about fifty colleges reject more students than they accept (Steinberg, 2002). Because of this situation, selective colleges and, even more so, elite colleges, are viewed as rare commodities, making them more appealing and the competition for them greater. According to Bourdieu (1984), the consumption of rare goods, those goods that are in shorter supply in the market, is considered the consumption of the most legitimate cultural goods. The scarcer something is, the more "legitimate" it is and the more association it has with high culture. The more widely available something is, the more it is viewed as being an item of "popular taste." The commodities that fall somewhere in between are considered of "middle-brow" taste (Bourdieu, 1984, p. 16). This theory also helps explain why competition for as well as prestige of degrees from, say, Middlebury College and the University of Phoenix, differ. The degree from Middlebury College is considered more prestigious and more authentic.

Consumers of elite education also see the private benefits it yields. Parents certainly want to see a return on their investment in their children's education and upbringing until this point (Robbins, 2006), but students and parents are well aware of other returns that could come as a result of a brand-name degree. Research supports the idea that where someone attends college and one's future are clearly linked. For example, where one attends college significantly influences how much education one will eventually attain (McDonough, 1997). Multiple studies have found that one's institution of higher education can affect one's future education, occupation, and income as well as a number of nonsocioeconomic outcomes such as tolerance, civic participation, and happiness (Karen, 2002).

The increasing competition for spots in selective higher education institutions and the price attached to them are parts of a larger debate. The higher education community is increasingly concerned that, as a result of viewing higher education as a commodity, education is being interpreted as a private good with individual benefits and is therefore losing its value as a public good, a characteristic that it has had since its inception. American colleges and universities have never been seen as isolated ivory towers like their European counterparts, the models on which they were based—the English view of higher education for the elite classes and the German view of scholarly research as existing for its own sake (Brubacher and Rudy, 1997). Rather, they have been regarded as high watchtowers, playing a role in the advancement of American democracy (Brubacher and Rudy, 1997). This idea of higher education's preserving the basic needs of America and serving the public good has roots in the early colleges (Brubacher and Rudy, 1997). When Benjamin Franklin founded the University of Pennsylvania, then the College of Philadelphia, in the 1750s, he remarked that he wanted a "more useful culture of young minds" compared with the models at Oxford and Cambridge and that education should "serve mankind" (Kerr, 2001, p. 9).

Upper-Middle-Class Students and College Choice

A student's choosing the best college makes sense in the context of that student's family, friends, background, and cultural surroundings (McDonough, 1997). This section outlines consumer practices that upper-middle-class students engage in to increase their chances of admission to selective colleges. Private college counselors (or independent educational consultants) are an example of a consumer good that students and their parents purchase in the selective college market. With the increasing scarcity of places in the first-year classes of America's most elite institutions, consumers of higher education (that is, upper-middle-class students and their parents) have turned to this resource to help them access a rare commodity (McDonough, Korn, and Yamasaki, 1997). As the competition has increased for higher education, the strategies of economically advantaged students have evolved, in turn changing the nature of the competition (McDonough, Korn, and Yamasaki, 1997). This idea is based on Bourdieu's principle that in some areas people struggle over capital (particularly cultural capital because of its ability to influence future educational plans) (McDonough, Korn, and Yamasaki, 1997). Hiring private college counselors is one way that upper-middle-class students and their parents try to maximize their cultural capital and thus better their chances of gaining educational capital, as cultural practices and educational capital are directly linked (Bourdieu, 1984).

According to a survey of independent educational consultants conducted by McDonough, Korn, and Yamasaki (1997) and published in *The Review of Higher Education,* independent educational consultants conduct most of their work in the area of college admissions but also engage in high school and pre–high school advising (McDonough, Korn, and Yamasaki, 1997). When the survey was conducted, the average cost of a college counseling package, which most consultants offer, was $950, while the hourly charge was $86 and the average per visit charge was $150 (McDonough, Korn, and Yamasaki, 1997). The most powerful indicator of whether someone will use an independent education consultant is socioeconomic status. McDonough, Korn, and Yamasaki estimate that 40,500 students use private counselors, which in 1997 was four times higher than any previously recorded estimate.

Independent college counselors or consultants usually perform a range of functions for their clients. They may help complete college applications, coach for SATs, edit essays, and reduce stress and anxiety that students (and their parents) experience over the admissions process (McDonough, 1997). No matter the specific range of services each consultant offers, however, what they all have in common is that they provide individual attention (McDonough, 1997). Some students and parents perceive this attention as increasingly important because in a period when competition for admission to selective colleges is increasing, the amount of time each student can spend with his or her school's guidance counselor discussing college-related issues is decreasing as a result of the changing role and increasing responsibilities placed on guidance counselors in public high schools, even elite ones (Mathews, 1998).

Does hiring an independent educational consultant help with the actual admissions process? Do students gain access to places that they otherwise might not have without this service? The answer to these questions is unclear. What is clear, however, is that hiring an independent educational consultant positively influences the number of applications a student files, which in turn may bear on the ultimate outcome (McDonough, Korn, and Yamasaki, 1997). Admissions staff do not necessarily believe that the services of private counselors influence students' ultimate determination of the right school, but families do because the counselor introduces a wider range of options than the student otherwise would have had (McDonough, 1997).

In addition, the higher education admissions market includes other services such as SAT preparation classes. Stanley Kaplan's test preparation courses arose directly as a result of the increased competition for higher education and change in the market. Classes were offered as early as the 1950s. These services became extremely popular, and competitors such as the Princeton Review took hold in the 1980s (Steinberg, 2002). In addition, a large guidebook market includes texts that dispense advice on topics from writing college admissions essays to insider tips on how to scale the Ivy wall and gain access to America's selective colleges and universities (Steinberg, 2002).

These upper-middle-class students and their parents also try to maximize cultural capital and thus their chance of college acceptance through other schooling opportunities. Some parents try to increase their child's cultural capital well before the junior year of high school, when the admissions process is imminent. The desire to set one's child up for success can, in extreme cases, start from a very young age—or even from birth. In recent decades, pressure to give an edge to the disadvantaged has been replaced by an intensification of the privileged wanting to maintain their status (Karabel, 2005). And it can be seen in the ferocious competition for the right kindergarten, an intense process for which parents sometimes hire independent educational consultants (Karabel, 2005, p. 3).

The location of a high school is also important to many students and parents because of the potential value of this experience to a favorable outcome in college admissions. Most high schools and colleges are at best loosely coupled (McDonough, 1997), but a few schools (both public and private) have a tight coupling as a result of their college preparation and Advanced Placement (AP) classes, connection to particular high-status colleges, and efficient information flow about the college application and admission process (McDonough, 1997). Elite preparatory schools such as Groton, Exeter, and St. Paul's have historically had ties to the Big Three, and up until 1954 sent roughly two-thirds of their graduates to one of these schools (Karabel, 2005). *The Gate keepers* (Steinberg, 2002) describes a special relationship between Harvard-Westlake, a high school in California, and a counselor at Wesleyan who often recruits students from this school. Although an individual's academic achievement is a key factor in whether an individual attends college, the interaction between a student's social class and the high school's organizational context is central to the question of where an individual attends college (McDonough, 1997). Overall, the type of secondary school one attends and its location are associated with a student's college destination. For example, private schools are positively associated with college attendance, while rural schools are negatively associated (Karen, 2002)—which is why these parents pay attention not only to where their children go to college but also to high school, elementary school, and even preschool.

Another way that economic capital is exchanged for cultural capital is in the form of property taxes. Not all upper-middle-class parents give their students access to cultural capital through private school, but many spend just as much money accessing it in other ways. For example, Mathews's account (1998) of Mamaroneck High School in Westchester County, New York, which the author calls an elite high school, notes that in 1996 two families purchased houses next door to each other that were nearly identical in size and condition. Yet one family paid $540,000, while the neighbors paid $350,000. The reason for this discrepancy was that the higher-priced house had access to the Mamaroneck schools and the other did not (Mathews, 1998). With the college application in mind, parents also spend money on activities outside school that might help students gain even more cultural capital and further their chances of admission: music lessons, extracurricular activities, academic training, and athletics (Avery, Fairbanks, and Zeckhauser, 2003).

For students from upper-middle-class backgrounds applying for admission to selective institutions, practices such as working with college consultants, attending elite elementary and secondary schools, taking SAT preparation classes, engaging in activities outside school, and perhaps adding character-building (and therefore application-building) experiences have become the norm. They are cultural practices and can become expectations for members of a particular class. Both parents and peers dictate what it takes to be "the best." In *The Overachievers,* Robbins describes a student who feels that not only scoring high on the SAT but also taking a preparation class to help him with his task is the norm as a result of his cultural context. "Now he was on his way to spend three full hours in an SAT class, as he would every Thursday for the next month. He had scored well on the test in the spring, but when he heard about other Whitman students' higher scores—students he believed weren't as smart as he was—he resolved to take the test again" (Robbins, 2006, p. 29).

According to McDonough (1997), who draws on a model established by Hossler and Gallagher, college choice has three main stages: predisposition, when a student first decides when he or she will go to college; search, when the student looks for general information about college and forms opinions about different colleges; and choice, when the student narrows down his or her choices to a single college and decides to attend it. Socioeconomic status determines how students will approach each stage (McDonough, 1997).

Many students will be satisfied with their choices and the final outcome of the admissions process. In making the final college choice, however, the upper-middle-class population can also have a sense of entitlement. Although students and their families are fully aware of intense competition for places in higher education, students believe they are entitled to a particular type of college education, depending on their high school or family background (McDonough, 1997). This belief can result in parents' taking action when students do not get into the "best" or "right" school such as calling a counselor about "a friend of a client who is on the Board of Trustees, the interested field hockey coach, or the third cousin whose boss donated a science building" (Mathews, 1998, p. 23).

Sometimes a student's final college choice is different from that of his or her parent. Because parents of privileged students tend to be highly involved in the admissions process, this situation can be difficult for both parties. Robbins tells about a student whose final college choice was very different from his parents' choice in a story that appeared in *U.S.A. Today*, written by former M.I.T. Director of Admissions Marilee Jones. "Last April, a few weeks after sending the acceptance/rejection letters for the Class of 2006, I received a reply from a father of one of our applicants. It was curt and written on his corporate letterhead: 'You rejected my son. He's devastated. See you in court.' The very next day, I received another letter, but this time from the man's son. It read: 'Thank you for not admitting me to M.I.T. This is the best day of my life'" (Robbins, 2006, p. 222). Although they have similar backgrounds, parents and students do not always occupy the same mind-set. Parents and students may have different values, ideals, and cultural norms.

Parents and students take a number of measures to help students get into selective schools. Some of these practices are dictated by class standing. Ultimately, what parents and students are trying to achieve with these practices is to increase cultural capital, hoping it will lead to educational capital. Through these actions parent and student consumers gain a sense of agency in the competitive college admissions market.

The level of support for attending college seems to be inextricably linked to social class (Bourdieu, 1984; Lareau, 1987; Lamont and Lareau, 1988). As laid out in this section, the approach to college admissions by the parents in these two socioeconomic groups appears vastly different. If parents begin their experience with the college or university from such broadly different contexts, why would administrators put them into a broad category and regard them as all the same? Which parents sound the most like helicopters? One cannot assume that the experience of parents from different income and education levels approaches their child's experience in higher education in the same way. In general, the nature of the relationship between socioeconomic class and the parent-student dynamic once students are enrolled in an institution of higher education, especially for low-income, first-generation students, is an area where more research is needed.

Implications

PARENT PROGRAMMING AND SERVICES are not new phenomena among colleges and universities. It is the label of "helicopters," the emerging emphasis on generational characteristics, and the charge of intrusiveness that illustrate a change in both attitude and response toward college-parent relations. In fact, some institutions track parent relations back to the 1920s, and they harbor that relationship as a valued and integral campus tradition. For example, the University of Illinois at Urbana-Champaign boasts a Dads Association that was formed in 1922, with a Mothers Association incorporating one year later. Even then, the purpose of the associations was collaborative; the dads were committed to promoting "the general welfare of the University of Illinois at Urbana-Champaign, in cooperation with its faculty, staff, students, and parents" ("Moms and Dads Illinois: Dads Association," n.d.). Similarly, Illinois mothers pledged themselves to "the purpose of promoting the welfare and interest of the University and its students through services and open communications on campus and throughout the state" ("Moms and Dads Illinois: Moms Association," n.d.). Over the decades, the two groups have contributed to Illini scholarships, safety projects, campus beautification, library projects, and student groups ("Moms and Dads Illinois: Projects Benefiting Students," n.d.).

At Texas A&M, the Aggie Moms, known more formally as Texas A&M University's Mothers' Clubs, were first organized in 1922 and formed around the concept of contributing "in every way to the comfort and welfare of the boys and to cooperate with the faculty of the college in maintaining a high standard of moral conduct and intellectual attainment." In addition to these lofty goals, they provided an annual spread of fried chicken, sandwiches, pies, and cookies, and they raised funds to support student scholarships ("Federation of Texas A&M University Mothers' Clubs," 2007).

The Aggie Moms, like Illini parents, have been raising funds over the past eighty-plus years for such campus groups as the Aggie Band, the Corps of Cadets, the Endowment Fund for the Sterling C. Evans Library, Fish and Transfer Camps, and Peer Orientation Conferences, and hundreds of campus organizations have benefited from their support ("Federation of Texas A&M University Mothers' Clubs," 2007). Similarly, records from the Mothers' Club at Southern Methodist University, dating to 1926, report that the group has contributed over the years to planting trees on campus, purchasing band uniforms, and providing meals for campus-bound students on Thanksgiving (D. Kepler, personal communication, July 2007).

Certainly not all colleges and universities have had parent programs since the 1920s, and clearly parents' involvement on campus had a much different profile fifty or more years ago. For those schools with a long history of parent programming, annual and seasonal events were the norm, and many of their programs were gender-focused. Schools might have brought fathers to campus for a Dads Weekend in the fall that included a football game and barbecue, while mothers might have been invited to a spring tea with the president and his wife. The Illini Moms Day was first held in 1921, and the school's Dads Association officially started on November 6, 1922, concurrent with the first official Dads Weekend (Bahnmaier, 1988). Wells College in Aurora, New York, notes that a Parents Weekend was one of the first efforts after its Parents Club was started in 1951 (Detmold, 1989).

Little evidence has emerged that parent relations were considered problematic in these early years. Although the Aggie Moms' first meeting with faculty was reportedly met with laughter, when the mothers returned to campus a second time—and brought a picnic lunch for students—no objections were registered ("Federation of Texas A&M University Mothers' Clubs," 2007). It was during the tumultuous years of the late 1960s and 1970s that higher education's relationship with the family began to deteriorate. Schools started to examine the political correctness of inviting fathers and mothers separately to seasonal events, and at many institutions the result was to cancel them both. When Skidmore College voted to admit men in 1971, one of the casualties was the annual Happy Pappy Weekend, a father-daughter tradition that no longer seemed appropriate (Crocker, 1989).

Nationally, college students during the late 1960s and 1970s were exerting their independence, and the same outlook that yielded FERPA led colleges and universities to reevaluate their parent communications and activities. Some schools abandoned events for parents during the Vietnam War years, only to initiate or reintroduce programming for parents again in the 1980s and 1990s. Stanford University notes that Parents Weekend "died a sudden death in the late '60s when students weren't particularly eager to have their parents on campus, and families were a little uneasy about setting foot on the students' turf" (Duncan, 1989, p. 53). Later at Stanford, it was parents who, in 1984, proposed resuming Parents Weekend (Duncan, 1989).

At least one school, however, reacted to student war protests in the 1970s just the opposite way. The development of the Syracuse parents' office was a direct result of that era's turmoil. "Media reports (about campus protests) were exaggerated and unreliable. In their concern, parents often turned to administrators to learn what was going on. In response to this need, in 1972 Syracuse University established an office just for parents, one of the first of its kind in the country" (Severino, 1989, p. 69). According to the current parent office director at Syracuse, Colleen O'Connor Bench, the office was also conceived in response to cutbacks in federal funding for student aid. The requirement that parents help foot the bill for college made it clear that parents were a new, emerging customer in higher education.

Several years after the Vietnam era, parents at many schools began to call for involvement opportunities again. Parent programs and services developed slowly at first. Of 197 parent offices responding to a spring 2007 national survey, just over 12 percent reported that they date back to the 1970s or earlier. Another 6 percent originated between 1980 and 1985, and 8 percent were established between 1986 and 1989. In the 1990s, the concept of parent services took hold firmly, with nearly 17 percent of parent programs establishing offices between 1990 and 1995 and another 11 percent following in the last half of the 1990s. The trend continued after the turn of the century, with nearly 45 percent of today's parent offices opening their doors between 2000 and early spring 2007 (Savage, 2007).

Parent orientation programs, often mirroring student orientation programs, became one of the most common services (Savage, 2007). As early as 1984, family and parent concerns were identified as an important component of a school's orientation program (Upcraft, 1984). In partnership with student orientation programs, parent orientation seems to have evolved steadily since the 1980s, but there is earlier precedence for a parent orientation program. Once again serving as a pioneer in the field of family services, the University of Illinois may have been the first to introduce an orientation program specifically for parents when the Illini Mothers and Dads Associations offered "orientation activities" for parents from 1950 to 1959. After 1959, the university more formally brought parents into their orientation program (Bahnmaier, 1988).

In the formative years of parent services, college-parent communication was not controversial. Before the introduction of FERPA, student information was sent to the home address and, at least in some cases, addressed to the parents. Parents knew when grades and bills were sent because they landed in the home mailbox. Mass mailings, either personally addressed to parents or labeled "to the parents of . . . ." might address back-to-school messages from the president or invite families to moms or dads weekends. With societal and institutional changes in the 1960s and 1970s, however, those mailings became less frequent and were addressed to the student. By the mid-1980s, parents were becoming frustrated with the lack of information. The Princeton Parents Project, which surveyed ninety-one colleges and universities in 1985–1986, revealed that "parents wanted more information about their student's institution—from the institution. And they particularly wanted more personal communication in any form. They wanted the institution to show some appreciation for the sacrifices they were making to send their son or daughter to the school. They also wanted reassurance that the institution was, in fact, the best place for their child" (New, 1989, pp. 99–100). Throughout the 1990s, more schools added parent orientation programs or newsletters for parents, developed handbooks for parents, and paid more attention to the "family decision" of college selection.

Since 2000, changes have come even more rapidly in parent services. In 1999, a survey of colleges and universities indicated that most parent offices provided just one or two parent services or events. At that time, 43 percent of schools responding were offering a parent or family weekend and a third were

TABLE 1
Parent Services, 1999–2007

	1999	2003	2005	2007
What parent services does your office or institution provide for parents?				
Family Day/Weekend	43%	74.4%	96%	94.9%
Parent Orientation	35%	61.0%	97%	95.2%
Newsletter	33%	54.9%	56%	54.3%
Parents Council/Advisory Board	5%	36.6%	60%	65.4%
Fundraising	12%	43.9%	84%	85.2%
Welcome Week/Move-In	NA	7.3%	75%	73.8%
Handbook	31%	12.2%	75%	78.6%

Note: Surveys were conducted with schools that have parent services; 1999 survey listed only six programs or services, while 2007 survey listed fourteen.

offering parent orientation, but only 16 percent offered both. In 2007, on the other hand, almost all schools that provide parent services offered both a parent or family weekend and a parent orientation (95 percent offer both); 75 percent also offer family events on move-in day when students first arrive on campus. Given a list of fourteen common parent services, 96 percent indicated they provided five or more of those services (Savage, 2007).

Parent Services and Best Practices

At issue among student affairs staff and other higher education professionals is the outcome of parent services. Are such services helping parents find answers to their legitimate questions, or are they are opening the door to parents' intrusiveness on topics that students should be addressing themselves? Because the answer seems to be "both," the challenge is for colleges and universities to decide on the type of relationship they prefer to have with parents—a partnership, a clear separation, or something in between (Keppler, Mullendore, and Carey, 2005).

Best practices in parent programming, then, include components for not only educating parents on what is appropriate intervention but also helping them to understand why colleges and universities want students to handle their own college and university responsibilities. An intentional parent program with the purpose of student development is designed to provide advice on parenting a college student, relieve parents' common fears, proactively address issues and expect preemptive phone calls and e-mails, promote campus events and activities, and open dialogue between parents and students. The benefit of parental involvement should be two way, with some positive impact directed back to the institution in the form of parents' goodwill, advocacy, and potential funding.

In the late 1990s, the Office of New Student Orientation and Parent Programs at Northeastern University in Boston conducted a national review of approximately sixty colleges and universities to identify best practices in programming for parents and families of college undergraduates. In 2007, participants attending the annual Administrators Promoting Parent Involvement conference both endorsed and updated the original list to reflect new technology. According to that group, a comprehensive parent program for a college or university would have:

- A clearly written mission statement;
- Central coordination of campus events for parents and families;
- A parents' orientation program for parents of incoming students, reflecting the parental perspective on information offered at student orientation;
- Multiple campus events for parents, including but not limited to parents and families weekends and—move-in events;
- Other educational and social events and programs unique to the institution;
- A central, personal contact point for parents with phone number and e-mail address;
- An active and current Web site;
- An active parents' association or an active parents' council or advisory board;
- Outgoing publications such as newsletters, bulletins, and e-newsletters;
- A campus resource guide or handbook for parents;
- Special funds with parent input for use by funds-development programs, with fees or dues designated for support of student scholarships or other projects or services; and
- A defined and recurring assessment process to measure use of, satisfaction with, and success of programs and services.

In an age of information, around-the-clock services are available online from banks, health care providers, and insurance companies; we can shop online day or night, including holidays; we can look up phone numbers, search for answers to questions, and fill out job applications online. That expectation of always-available information extends to educational institutions and the services they provide. Consequently, just as higher education as a whole has been affected by new technologies, communications with parents also have changed significantly in recent years. The annual print version of a parent handbook and periodic snail-mail parent newsletters remain helpful, but they do not provide the timely information that parents demand. Parent Web pages, for example, have become a staple on college and university Web sites during the past fifteen years. In the early 1990s, few if any colleges offered Web sites for parents; indeed, colleges and universities at that time were struggling to design their institutional front page. In 2007, however, 95.8 percent of institutions with a parent program have a Web page for parents (Savage, 2007).

Similarly, online information and e-mail newsletters have increasingly become a basic expectation. Most of today's parents of college students have had close contact with their student's schools since kindergarten; the No Child Left Behind Act, in fact, promotes two-way involvement and communication. Grade school, middle school, and high school teachers and administrators now send parents their e-mail addresses, and many schools distribute weekly or monthly electronic newsletters. In the same vein, colleges and universities are finding value in developing parent listservs to keep parents updated on events and activities by sending a weekly or monthly electronic newsletter, and they repeat to parents the messages they send to students; 73 percent of colleges and universities providing parent services produce an e-mail newsletter (Savage, 2007).

A successful college e-mail newsletter, as described by the director of a parent program, "keeps parents/families connected to the University with advice on parenting a college student, important event/date information, and brief articles written specifically for parents from key campus offices." Another parent professional notes, "I think [our parent e-mail newsletter] assuages fears parents may have and preempts parent phone calls to the office." Yet another parent program director says, "I think [the e-mail newsletter] opens dialogue for parents/families with their children. Instead of, 'what did you make on xyz?' they can talk about what's going on, offer advice if needed, and see what is coming up" (Savage, 2007).

As the list of best practices indicates, parent programs should routinely provide a hotline number and e-mail response to parents' questions. In addition, some schools (20 percent) offer a chat room for parents to share comments among themselves, and still others are experimenting with parent blogs or message boards to discuss topics of concern. Northeastern University's Parents Corner Message Board, for example, gives parents a place to ask questions and receive responses from the university's parent office and from other parents ("Northeastern University Parent Message Board," 2007).

Technology has provided useful tools for schools to provide educational workshops and programs to families at a distance without the need to come to campus. North Carolina State University has produced a series of live Web casts that address issues specific to parents of freshmen, sophomores, and transfer students, as well as programs on alcohol, depression, and career planning ("N.C. State University," 2007).

Southern Methodist University posts two- to six-minute videos in a "Parents Guide to the First Year" section on its Web page as a way to help parents understand the student experience at SMU (Southern Methodist University, 2007). The videos are geared to the season, with late-summer segments that focus on the start of school and transition stages. As the year progresses, videos feature student events to let parents share campus traditions and events.

The University of Minnesota has developed online courses for parents that offer information on the topics of college drinking and student financial management. Through a series of lessons, parents taking the courses receive information on national trends on the topics, campus resources, and talking points for working with college-age students on these issues.

If parents are served well and feel included in the campus community, they will bestow more on the institution than just their children and tuition payments:—they will contribute their time, goodwill, and monetary gifts. Parent volunteers can add value to institutional programs. One school cites its parent-to-parent calling program as a best practice: parents of upperclassmen make phone calls to families of first-year students to discuss the transition to college. If problem areas are identified, staff follow up with the family to ensure the student's and parents' needs are met. Another university notes that nearly 20 percent of their parents volunteer as hosts and greeters for special activities; as panelists and presenters for Family Weekend, seminars, and admissions events; and as support for staff during major campus events (Savage, 2007).

Among schools that raise funds from parents, the results can benefit targeted programs or supplement an entire department's funding. One school noted, "We will raise over $1 million from non-alumni parents this year for the Annual Fund. We also cultivate major gifts from parents" (Savage, 2007). In many cases, fundraising is filtered through a parents' council or parents' advisory group that also helps by mentoring students in career development and assists with recruitment.

Today's Parents: Mentors or Machines?

Despite the media's portrayals of today's parents as "helicopter parents," not all parents qualify under the definition of highly involved and intrusive. Parents, like students, fit a broad profile. Some may be inappropriately involved, some may be helpfully involved as needed, and some would be defined as distant or negligent. So who are the helicopter parents? The ones who can afford helicopters? Maybe. Or they may be the parents who have "consumer skills" and who have been successful in the past in their efforts to obtain extra benefits for their children. Or they may be the parents who went to college themselves and have certain expectations. Or they might be parents who simply have not received sufficient information from their child's school about the policies and procedures in place to handle the issues that are worrisome to parents during the college years. They may feel they must be involved to ensure that someone is overseeing the system.

As mentioned earlier, parents of today's college students share a number of common concerns: they worry about college finances, their student's health and safety, and their student's academic success. A review of data tracking reports from a number of colleges and universities, which record parent contacts and the concerns parents are expressing, shows that these concerns are among the most frequent topics of phone calls, e-mails, and in-person questions received by parent offices. Similarly, when college parents have responded to surveys asking them to name their greatest concern regarding their students, their answers reflect the same topics—finances, health and safety, and academics—although the order of priority may change from one school to the next.

The time of year and the student's year in college make a difference in the questions that parents ask. For parents of first-year students, questions during the weeks preceding a move to campus tend to focus on housing and billing details: "When can students move in?" "When does the meal plan begin?" "Can students have a microwave?" "Does the school provide bookshelves?" "When will bills be sent?" "Can we pay in installments?"

As students progress through college, the detailed questions about dining, housing, and billing fade, and the concerns turn to measures of success: "Is my student's sociology major going to relate to a career?" "With a 3.0 GPA, will my student be able to get into law school?" "Is there someone who can help my student find an internship?" "Who can talk to my student about graduate programs?"

At least some of these parental concerns are understandable. It is not unusual, nor would most higher education professionals consider it offensive, for parents to contact their child's school with questions about deadlines for financial aid applications, reports of a student's health emergency, or fears about a student who has gone missing. Frustrations arise among staff and administrators, however, when parents do their student's work—contacting a faculty member to request an extension on an assignment, seeking an advisor's suggestions on changing majors, or asking how to replace a lost identification card. At Syracuse University, 2006–2007 data show that although a large number of contacts would be considered normal and appropriate, about 45 percent of parents' office contacts were "to help resolve a situation that their student has been unable to resolve." These situations were most frequently roommate issues but also included academic concerns. "My son's professor gave him a C on a paper that we saw him work very hard on over Thanksgiving vacation, and I know he deserves at least a B" (C. Bench, personal communication, July 2007).

Directors of parent programs, however, point out that the calls they receive may not reflect the overall picture of parent-college contacts. It is likely, for example, that the financial aid office receives the vast majority of calls from parents about finance matters. An academic advisor, on the other hand, probably receives more calls from parents about advising issues than the parent office handles (L. Stevens, personal communication, July 2007). Consequently, it can be hard for any one office to fully understand the scope of parents' concerns and contacts. Nevertheless, the consensus is that parents today are indeed involved.

Parents themselves acknowledge that they are more involved than their own parents were a generation ago. When asked about their level of involvement or communication with their child compared to the involvement or communication they had with their parents when they were in college, 78.7 percent of University of Minnesota parents said they are "more involved" or "much more involved" (Savage, 2006). A similar question posed by College Parents of America, an advocacy association for parents of college students, in a national survey showed that 81 percent of respondents identified themselves as "more or much more involved" than their own parents had been (College Parents of America, 2007).

Parents' questions may also reflect their own educational background, culture, or financial standing. Parents who did not themselves attend college are likely to ask more detailed questions or try to understand basic terminology: "Are students supposed to go home on the weekend?" "What is the bursar's office?" "Does someone help my student register for classes?"

Despite parents' level of involvement and their interest in their student's college experience, parents do not necessarily know what constitutes appropriate involvement and what would fall into the realm of inappropriate involvement. A few institutions have taken the step of spelling out criteria for desired parental outcomes to help parents understand the college experience, support their student's academic and personal growth, and be involved appropriately with their student and with the institution. Just as colleges and universities create learning outcomes for students as a way to define competencies and skills to be mastered during the college years, parental outcomes can do the same for family members. In 2004, the National Association of Student Personnel Administrators (NASPA) and the American College Personnel Association (ACPA) called for a new way of looking at postsecondary learning that considers how and where student learning occurs, tracks that learning is taking place, and establishes the desired outcomes of learning (Keeling, 2004). Western Washington University used *Learning Reconsidered* guidelines to develop a set of learning outcomes for its first-year students and then created a set of parent outcomes that reinforce the student outcomes by defining a guideline for parents in understanding their role during the college years (see Exhibit 1).

By developing a list of parent outcomes, institutions have a format to think through and articulate their goals for parental involvement not only to parents but also to students and staff. Just as development of student outcomes requires input and collaboration from faculty, staff, and students, so does the process of determining a set of parent outcomes. Outcomes are individualized to the institution and its mission, reflect the values of the college or university, are flexible enough to reflect the diversity of the student body and the families of those students, and can be assessed.

Challenges in Working with Parents

Parent program staff identify several areas of ongoing and emerging concerns in their daily work of developing and delivering services for parents. One of the most significant is the broad range of responsibilities the office requires; staff members are expected to extend their services well beyond their areas of expertise. Most parent programs are situated in a student affairs/student development office (53 percent) or in an advancement/fundraising or alumni office (30 percent). Consequently, most parent program staff come to their jobs with a student affairs background or fundraising skills and experience (Savage, 2007). A typical parent office, however, requires staff members to provide good customer service, written and oral communication, event planning, large- and small-group presentations, budget management, personal and family counseling, Web site management, marketing, public relations, and fundraising.

Increasingly, the distinction between student affairs–based programs and fundraising programs is blurred. Offices that are housed in an advancement, foundation, or alumni office with a proven record for fundraising are being given responsibility for communicating student development information through Web sites, e-mail and print newsletters, and educational workshops. Nearly a

EXHIBIT 1
Western Washington University: Desired Outcomes for Students and Parents

Student Outcomes: New Student Services

Learning Outcomes

Over the course of the first year, students should:

- Establish an appreciation for the life of the mind.
- Recognize campuswide resources, both academic and service related.
- Demonstrate competence and confidence in accessing resources.
- Be aware of the components of a healthy lifestyle.
- Articulate the qualities of a responsible member of the campus community and the role they play as individuals.
- Understand the attributes necessary to be a successful student and engaged in one's own learning.
- Articulate their academic goals in relation to the University's mission and curriculum.

Affective Outcomes

Over the course of the first year, students should:

- Develop a feeling of belonging and community.
- Be confident in using campus resources.
- Demonstrate self-efficacy.
- Be optimistic regarding their ability to be successful in their academic career.

Parent Outcomes: Family Outreach

Learning Outcomes

Focused on assisting students persist and succeed at WWU, family outreach programs and services are provided for the parents and family members of current students with the purpose of:

- Developing an understanding of the academic and classroom opportunities available at WWU and the application of that learning.
- Recognizing campuswide resources that support student success and how to access those services.
- Understanding the complex nature of students' academic experience and the role they can play as mentors.
- Developing an awareness of the political climate that higher education operates in at the state and federal levels.

EXHIBIT 1 *(Continued)*

Affective Outcomes
Over the course of a student's career at WWU, parents and family members should:
• Develop an affinity for WWU.
• Develop a feeling of belonging and community.

Source: Carey, 2004, 2005.

third of the advancement-based offices now are hosting educational workshops for parents, and three-fourths are responsible for responding to parents' e-mail questions and for overseeing a Web site for parents. Similarly, individuals with a student affairs background are expected to develop or support a fundraising plan to solicit donations from families (Savage, 2007). Moreover, that reporting structure dictates how the job will be approached: Is the underlying purpose of the program to raise funds? If so, that goal influences how programs and services will be delivered, and certain parents (and their students) may expect more privileges from the institution. Is the main purpose to promote students' success through a student development office? In that case, communications and services will probably be more service oriented and more evenly distributed.

In addition, emerging technologies raise the performance bar for parental program staff; many professionals staffing parent offices (26 percent of survey respondents) cited their Web site as the "weakest link" of their program. They understand that a Web site should be dynamic and interactive, but many said they do not have the time or skills to design and regularly update the site. The expertise that makes a good parent program professional tends not to align with development of the Web site. Consequently, the site is often turned over to and managed by a central technology office, which may not ultimately benefit the parent office. As one respondent noted, "The University Web project has relegated [the parent site] to a very low priority." Some said that they do not have the political power to get a link from the institution's home page (Savage, 2007).

Weighed against student needs, faculty expectations, funding priorities, alumni interests, and administrative priorities, parent offices do indeed lack political power. When asked for advice for new professionals in the field, parent program staff frequently noted the need for collaboration:

*It is extremely important to collaborate with other campus depart-
ments on campus—get a point person to go to in each department—sometimes you have to give more on your end in order to
get the desired outcomes, especially when the project is new. After-
ward, you will have campus community people wanting to be on
the same team as you. . . .*

*I think to be successful it is important for a parent relations pro-
fessional to get out and meet with the various offices on campus that
have a need to communicate with and "touch" parents—to coor-
dinate activities and programs for parents in a holistic way. . . .*

It's all about relationships [Savage, 2007].

The Bottom Line: Cost

If parent services help families understand critical information about student
development and about the institution, help them support their student's
retention, graduation, and success during the college years, and provide the
potential for extra funds for the institution, is the outcome worth the expense?
What does it cost to provide parent services? Like any other program in higher
education, different institutions devote different amounts to parent services.
As the field of parent relations emerges, office budgets are gaining support,
and parent professionals are becoming more valued. Still, they may be considered a bargain when viewed through the lens of value to the institution.

More than three-fourths of parent program staff members work with the program part time, with 56 percent devoting twenty hours per week or less to parent services. In many cases, the role of dealing with parents is coupled with other
responsibilities such as alumni, enrollment management, new student programs,
external relations, or church relations. The salary range is vast, varying from less
than $30,000 annually (for half-time staff and graduate assistants in the position)
to more than $100,000; the median in 2007 ranged from $50,000 to $59,000.
The majority of parent staff have earned a master's degree or higher, and the range
of their educational backgrounds is as extensive as their employment experience.
Undergraduate degrees were most often in majors such as psychology, sociology,
English, education, journalism and communications, business, and the fine arts,

but they also represented hard sciences (biology and chemistry), languages, math, history, political science, and even religion and criminology.

In terms of the master's degree, half the degrees are related to education, including student affairs or student personnel, higher education administration, community education, physical education, and elementary and secondary education. Also represented, however, are counseling, business, communications, psychology, the arts, the sciences (biomedical and chemistry degrees), and religion. Above the master's level, almost all degrees are focused on education, and the median salary rises to $60,000 to $69,000 (Savage, 2007).

Excluding salaries and fringe benefits, parent services offices receive budgets as high as $438,000 and as low as zero. The highest budgets reflect offices that include parent orientation budgets, and the majority of those funds are raised through programming or parent memberships. Offices with zero budgets typically note that they do not receive central funding and must cover all expenses through program fees or donations from parents. Among offices that receive their entire budget from central funding, the average operating budget (minus salary and fringe benefits) was $32,639 in 2007.

When Do Colleges Need Parents?

Working with parents is not a one-way street. Aside from the fundraising benefits that colleges and universities may gain through a parent relations program, parents provide a means of reinforcing institutional messages in ways the institution cannot. Most colleges and universities, for example, have tried every tactic available to reduce college drinking, to talk about campus safety, and to promote a healthy lifestyle. Despite all this research and these efforts, however, parents question the institutional response to drinking, safety, and other student issues such as mental health, excessive use of credit cards, and sexuality.

By bringing parents into the educational equation on personal, social, and economic issues, administrators gain a partner who has the most at stake in their student's well-being. Moreover, parents can add to institutional messages by infusing them with family or personal history. Increasingly, schools consider parents as not only an audience but also a stakeholder in the messages they deliver to students.

Recommendations

WHEN TRADITIONAL-AGE STUDENTS come to college, especially those with college-educated parents, they bring with them a family support system. Their parents have been their best advisors throughout the K–12 years. Students as well as their parents are comfortable with that relationship, and we believe colleges and universities can gain more by developing a plan to work with family dynamics than by fighting against them.

At the beginning of this monograph, we provided our definition of parental involvement and talked about five primary factors—generation, cost of college, use of technology, changes in parenting, and demographics—that may contribute to the phenomenon of parental involvement. Our definition and these factors connect directly and indirectly to the recommendations we offer for administrators and staff as they review their current parent relations and consider next steps. We defined parental involvement as showing interest in the lives of their students in college, gaining more information about college, knowing when and how to appropriately provide encouragement and guidance to their students, connecting with the institution, and potentially retaining that institutional connection beyond the college years.

Generation

We noted that students have been categorized generationally and treated as a broad population. Similarly, their parents have been categorized generationally. When Millennials first arrived in college in 2000, their parents neatly fit into the population of Baby Boomers. In the next few years, the majority of college parents will be GenXers (born in the early 1960s or later). Contemporary parent programs have been developed with Boomer parents in mind, and the growing question is, "What needs to change for GenX parents?"

No matter their generational designation, though, the common characteristic of today's college parents is that they raised Millennial students. Their students' shared experiences include technology, the No Child Left Behind Act, school choice, an appreciation for diversity, a goal of attending college, and a close relationship with parents. The parents also shared those experiences through their children. Most of the concerns of Baby Boomer parents are the same as those of GenX parents.

A few notable differences exist, however. Baby Boomers grew up with an underlying belief that if a system did not work for them, they would work to change it. Their philosophy fell along the lines of "anything should be possible." GenXers, on the other hand, always had choices—from cable TVs with multiple viewing options to alternative high schools and create-your-own majors in college; their outlook is "anything should be available." If Boomers are dissatisfied with something about the college or university their student attends, they are likely to advocate for change. If GenXers are unhappy with the institution, they may simply encourage their student to find another option. Institutions should consider the transfer factor from both sides—how to encourage students to persist and how to work more successfully with transfer students and their families. Already some schools are developing a parent session for transfer orientation programs.

Most important to the discussion about generational factors, however, is the point that was made earlier about cultural influence. What really matters is not when the parents or their students were born: the family experience as a whole is most critical. Parents who have been to college themselves and know the system provide support in different ways from parents who have never been to college. Ethnic and cultural factors influence parenting styles.

Cost of College

With little evidence that the cost of college is likely to go down, parents look for value. The No Child Left Behind Act prepared parents for measurable outcomes, and they expect similar standards from higher education. They compare colleges and universities in terms of housing options, meal plans, and other quality-of-life factors, but they are also keenly aware of time to graduation, career placement, and the perceived value of a diploma from the institution. They ask for specifics in terms of how many students graduate in four years, how many students in their child's major get a job in the field, how likely their student is to get into a top graduate program with a degree from the institution. Institutions need to be prepared for these questions during the admissions process, as these issues will come up as their student progresses through college.

The value of the education extends beyond just cost to educational quality and access. Parents expect instructors to meet basic standards, and an instructor with an accent is seen not as an enriching international opportunity but as a barrier to their student's education. A professor whose teaching method is purely lecture may face criticism for not acknowledging multiple learning styles. The concept of adjunct faculty who may have practical knowledge but not teaching credentials could raise concerns.

Because today's parents were encouraged by No Child Left Behind to consult with K–12 educators, they may be increasingly likely to expect they will have access to college instructors. Few current faculty are prepared for parent contact. If their immediate response is to dismiss the parent, administrators can expect hostile phone calls. Part of a comprehensive plan for parent relations should include informing faculty about the role of parents in their students' lives, with some suggestions about how to respond to parents. Faculty members can, for example, explain that they would like to talk the issue over directly with the student and encourage the parent to let the student know that. They can talk about classroom procedures and assignments in general terms without addressing the individual student's performance. They can refer parents to online information such as a syllabus or course outline. They can outline where and how the student can receive tutoring or other assistance.

Use of Technology

Technology has changed everything about education: how students learn, how instructors teach, how we provide services, and when information is available.

We cannot expect that technology will not affect how students relate to others, including their parents. As we incorporate technology in all aspects of teaching, learning, and communication, we should recognize that it provides a cost-effective means of relating to all our constituencies, including parents. By developing targeted messages to parents, we can proactively answer their most common questions, help them understand the education they are paying for, and incorporate them effectively and appropriately into the college community. As noted earlier, most parents are comfortable with technology and most use it fluently. In cases of a technology divide, it is important to weigh the value of putting information out for parents who can access it so that more time is available to address individual questions from those who cannot. For example, an institutional crisis plan could allow parents to sign up for text messages alerting the campus community to an emergency situation and direct recipients to a Web site for more information. Such a plan allows the majority of parents to find the information they want and need quickly.

When considering the use of technology in communications, it is important to also consider that communication styles differ somewhat for Boomers and GenXers. Boomers like to receive information in simple, short, straightforward, organized formats. They like bullets and PowerPoint presentations. GenXers prefer information that is delivered quickly. They want random access to information (hypertexting), and they like graphic illustration more than step-by-step instructions. During the transition years to the time when most parents will be GenXers, it may be useful to present information in multiple ways—written and bulleted information for Boomer parents and multimedia presentations for GenXers.

Changes in Parenting

As families begin their student's transition to college, parents and students alike make decisions about how they will relate differently to one another. Colleges and universities know this change will happen and that it is normal. The question becomes how institutions respond to this knowledge. Do they discuss it? Ignore it? Or facilitate it by helping parents and students understand it?

A significant piece of this quandary is that educators should expand their view of student development by learning more about attachment theory as an alternative, or complement, to separation-individuation. If administrators understand the value of parental involvement and the positive effects this relationship can have on a student's growth, it may quell their fears about the timeline for students' individuation. Of course, some parental behavior is disruptive. Using the attachment framework to understand the relationship between college students and their parents, however, will help administrators support all traditional-age students, especially female students. We believe that attachment theory should also be taught in student development classes as part of the standard curriculum. Graduate students in student affairs should learn about the new model and how it may inform the traditional theory of separation-individuation.

As mentioned earlier, we believe the research on attachment theory provides a necessary challenge to the traditional model of separation-individuation (Chickering and Reisser, 1993). As it is such a popular text in the field of student development and student affairs, this shift in thinking about relationships holds implications for those who work directly with students (Taub, 1997). We also believe that the literature on attachment would provide a good alternative theory to Howe and Strauss (2000, 2003) and would allow administrators to reduce their reliance on this source.

Institutions can respond to and build on new parenting relationships through the development of parent outcomes along with the student outcomes they promote, and by considering parents as a primary, or at least very important secondary, constituency. In an era when the legal system and parents decide what the relationship between students and the university should be, the university should have a say in what it wishes this ideal relationship to be, including the relationship between parents and the institution.

Demographics

Parent programs that have been up and running for several years have developed methods to meet the needs of their majority population of parents, and many are now beginning to consider the needs of underserved populations.

In fact, the research and assessment provided by parent offices contribute to an increased understanding and support of the majority college student population, which is frequently white, residential, traditional-age students whose parents have been involved throughout their lives, and primarily students whose parents have a college degree.

But what about the students—and their families—who do not fit that profile? Commuter students, transfer students, students who are parents themselves, first-generation college students, or first-generation Americans? Are these students placed at a double disadvantage because their parents do not seek out these services and information? Or because their parents cannot understand the information directed to that majority population of parents?

First-generation students and those from working-class families can find the transition to college particularly difficult. Just as their cultural background might distinguish their children from other college students, their identity as college students often differentiates them from their community and their family (Rendon, Garcia, and Person, 2004). They lack the skills and information about managing the college experience that is shared when family members have college experience (Rendon, Garcia, and Person, 2004). For commuter students, it can be difficult for parents to even understand why college presents new situations for their students; after all, they are still eating the same foods, sleeping in the same bed, and working at the same after-school job as they were in high school. Students whose parents do not speak English as a first language struggle to interpret college information for their parents, and students may not even know the words in their parents' language for "financial aid," "syllabus," "study group," or "registrar's office."

As schools look to the future, they are challenged to extend their parent services to these underserved populations. Increasingly, new issues are likely to emerge as more colleges and universities plan to work with different cultural and ethnic groups. Some parents, based on religious or moral principles, are unwilling to allow their children to live on campus. In Latino families, young unmarried women are encouraged to stay close to home; consequently, Latina college students are more likely to enroll in a nearby college and live at home (Rendon, Garcia, and Person, 2004).

In recent years, institutions have begun to look more carefully at how they communicate to different audiences in their parent populations. Several institutions translate printed materials into the languages of their largest non-English-speaking families. The College of St. Catherine, a Catholic women's college with a growing multicultural student population, for example, has developed videos for parents specific to Hmong, Latino, and Somali groups to help them understand the college experience their daughters will receive. Extensive research before production of the videos allowed the school to address the cultural issues of greatest concern to each population, and the videos feature students who speak the parents' language and discuss concerns they know their own parents had about college (D. Hauer, personal communication, August 22, 2007).

In some cases, culture or background may affect not only the kinds of questions a parent asks but also how parents are likely to contact the college or university. Syracuse University's Parents Office recently conducted a study to find out whether parent populations differ in terms of which office they called when they had questions. The results showed no differences in a parent's class, gender, or ethnicity related to the office a parent calls first with a question; a difference is apparent, however, based on the parent's financial need. A difference is also apparent for parents of first-generation students (Syracuse University Parents Office, July 2005).

For the majority of Syracuse parents, the initial call typically goes to the parents' office or directly to a target office, which is identified as the office that can solve the problem. Among parents of first-generation students or those with greater financial need, however, the first call is more likely to go to a "sponsoring office," defined as a multicultural office or a special support office, or to a financial aid advisor or another office where the student feels he or she has significant support.

At Syracuse, then, the parent office has developed intentional working relationships with sponsoring offices to provide better information about families to the staff in those sponsoring offices. The goal in improving these relationships is to work jointly across campus to establish rapport with the family, build families' skills related to college, and reinforce messages from the parent office about the role of parents' support in students' success (Syracuse University Parents Office, 2005).

Even as the popular Howe and Strauss (2000, 2003) say, one of the characteristics of the so-called Millennials is that they are diverse. One in five Millennials has a parent who is an immigrant (Oblinger, 2003). In addition, students from low-income families represent a growing population of our society's voters, taxpayers, and parents ("Higher Education for Students from Low Income Families," 2007), which may lead to even more diversity among higher education's student body. What will these projections mean for the future of parent relations, in terms of parent-student relationships, and the relationship of parents to the institution? When working with parents, administrators need to make sure that middle-class and upper-middle-class standard of behavior do not dictate institutional policy, as they have in K–12 education (Lareau, 1987). We recommend that parent programs and college administrators keep diversity at the forefront when thinking about serving today's students and their parents.

Even though some parents have the ability to donate resources to the institution above and beyond tuition dollars—and we do encourage institutions to cultivate this relationship for fundraising purposes—services for parents need to be targeted at and accessible to all parents, regardless of their income and donations. Administrators should regularly assess their programs to make sure that this goal is being met.

In addition, we recommend that colleges take on the role of working with parents before students matriculate, the parents of first-generation college students in particular. Why should high schools and college access programs do most of the work to reach out to these parents and educate them about how they can best support their student during the college application process and beyond? Higher education should take more responsibility for working with this group of parents and helping them to supplement their lack of cultural capital (Cabrera and La Nasa, 2001).

We also recommend that more research be conducted on the experiences of college students and parents from lower socioeconomic classes. Currently, the parent-student relationship for parents and students from middle and upper-middle classes is well known. What does the experience look like for lower-income students whose parents did not to go college? We know how significant a role parents can play in the lives of first-generation college students in the college admission process. We also know that first-generation students report "too little" parental involvement in their academic and social lives at college (Higher Education Research Institute, 2008). But what does the experience of these students and their parents really look like? In what ways are these parents involved?

In addition, more research could specifically be conducted about how the parent-student relationship affects retention. According to attachment theory, students may become part of new college communities without separating from the past. How does attachment theory challenge what we know about retention and Tinto's model (1993) in particular? How might parents be helpful in retention?

Conclusion

The majority of parents, particularly at selective colleges, have their own college-going experience, and they are inclined to advise their student about how to be successful. To expect that family relationship to change overnight, just because the student has turned eighteen or taken up residence on campus, is unrealistic.

Colleges and universities are most successful in working with parents when they define, explain, and support an appropriate role for parents during the college years. That role should be based on developmental theory, but it should take into account more than traditional student development theory and research. It should also include human development theory and a broad view in looking out for all students—women, nonresidential students, students of color, and nontraditional students. And we must keep in mind that parents should not be expected to innately understand the theory we operate under. They need to be educated about the developmental stages their student will undergo during the college years.

As we showed earlier, colleges and universities are increasingly looking at the role of parents in students' success. Every year, more institutions develop or formalize parent services. The benefits of these services extend beyond simply satisfying those vocal parents who make demands of colleges and universities to educating parents about the college experience they are financing. Parents also are becoming valuable partners in reinforcing our messages to students, and they are becoming major institutional donors. Our overarching recommendation, then, is that colleges and universities should have a mission-driven parent program that reflects the culture of the institution and the goals of student development. How that looks will be different based on the size of the institution, whether students are more likely to live on campus or live at home, whether the school is public or private, and where the parent program is housed in the institution.

Although the media have largely grouped parents into the broad category of "helicopter parents," it is important for both administrators and researchers to remember that this image represents only an extreme group and that parents, and their individual relationships with their students, are as varied as the students themselves. Different families may require different responses or treatments from the institution. If policy and practice are designed to serve only one type of parent—namely, parents who are eager to be involved—they may leave out others such as parents of first-generation college students who could provide an important source of support for their students in college.

Appendix: Resource Guide

To learn more about how colleges and universities have responded to the phenomenon of parental involvement, we recommend the following sources.

Organizations

APPI—Administrators Promoting Parent Involvement

This annual conference of parent program directors and staff has been meeting since 1996.

Contact: Susan Brown, Office of Parent and Family Programs, 101 Ell Hall, Northeastern University, 360 Huntington Avenue, Boston, MA 02115. Phone: (617) 373-3868; e-mail: s.brown@neu.edu

NASPA Parent and Family Relations Knowledge Community

This group, affiliated with NASPA, identifies and shares current research, best practices, and opportunities for new research in the area of college parenting.

Contact: National Association of Student Personnel Administrators, 1875 Connecticut Avenue, NW, Suite 418, Washington, DC 20009. Phone: (202) 265-7500.

National Orientation Directors Association Parent and Family Network

This group in NODA addresses the special orientation and transition programming needs of parents and family members of new college and university students and develops orientation formats and programs to accommodate parents and family members.

Contact: Ann Hower, Director of the Office of New Student Programs, University of Michigan at Ann Arbor, Ann Arbor, MI 48109. Phone: (734) 764-6413; e-mail: ahower@umich.edu

College Parents of America

A national membership association dedicated to advocating and to serving on behalf of current and future college parents.

Contact: College Parents of America, 2000 North 14th Street, Suite 800, Arlington, VA 22201-2540. Phone: (888) 761-6702; e-mail: info@ collegeparents.org

University Parent

This company produces institution-specific guides, e-newsletters, and comprehensive Web sites in partnership with universities across the United States for parents of college students.

Contact: University Parent, 4845 Pearl East Circle, Suite 101, Boulder, CO 80301. Phone: (720) 327-1628; e-mail: sarah@universityparent.com

Web Sites

Message Board
Northeastern University, Office of Parent and Family Programs
http://messageboard.chatuniversity.com/neuparent/

Web Site
Southern Methodist University, Parent Program
http://www.smu.edu/audience/parents/

Parent Handbook
University of North Carolina, Carolina Parent Program
http://parents.unc.edu/publications.php?action=handbook

Parental Involvement
University of Denver, Parents Program
http://www.parents.du.edu/involving/

Volunteer Opportunities for Parents
North Carolina State University, Parents and Family Services
http://www.ncsu.edu/for_parents/volunteer/

Online Workshops and Guides
University of Minnesota, University Parent Program
http://www.parent.umn.edu/workshops.php

Weblog
Calvin College, The Parent Connection
http://www.calvin.edu/weblogs/window

Diversity Video
College of St. Catherine
http://minerva.stkate.edu/offices/administrative/mips.nsf/pages/
recruitment_retention_videos/

National Survey of College and University Parent Programs, 2007
http://www.parent.umn.edu/ParentSurvey07.pdf

Parent Practices Database
NASPA Parent and Family Relations Knowledge Community
http://www.naspa.org/communities/kc/page.cfm?kcpageID=160andkcid=23

Selected Publications

Daniel, B. V., and Scott, B.,R. (2001). *Consumers, adversaries, and partners: Working with the families of undergraduates.* San Francisco: Jossey-Bass.

Keeling, R. (Ed.). (2004). *Learning reconsidered: A campus-wide focus on the student experience.* Washington, DC: National Association of Student Personnel Administrators and American College Personnel Association.

Keppler, K., Mullendore, R., and Carey, A. (2005). *Partnering with the parents of today's college students.* Washington, DC: National Association of Student Personnel Administrators.

Weiss, L. J. (Ed.). (1989). *Parents programs: How to create lasting ties.* Washington, DC: Council for Advancement and Support of Education.

References

ABC News (2005, October 20). *Do "helicopter moms" do more harm than good?* Retrieved October 30, 2007, from http://abcnews.go.com/2020/Health/story?id=1237868&page=1.

Allen, S., and Stoltenberg, C. D. (1995). Psychological separation of older adolescents and young adults from their parents: An investigation of gender differences. *Journal of Counseling and Development, 73*(5), 542–546.

Arnett, J. J. (1994). Are college students adults? Their conceptions of the transition to adulthood. *Journal of Adult Development, 1*(4), 213–224.

Arnett, J. J. (2000a). Emerging adulthood: A theory of development from the late teens through the twenties. *American Psychologist, 55*(5), 469–480.

Arnett, J. J. (2000b). High hopes in a grim world: Emerging adults' views of their futures and "Generation X." *Youth and Society, 31*(3), 267–286.

Arnett, J. J. (2006). Emerging adulthood: Understanding the new way of coming of age. In J. J. Arnett and J. L. Tanner (Eds.), *Emerging adults in America: Coming of age in the 21st century* (pp. 3–19). Washington, DC: American Psychological Association.

Astin, A., and Oseguera, L. (2004). The declining "equity" of American higher education. *Review of Higher Education, 27*(3), 321–341.

Attinasi, L. C. (1989). Getting in: Mexican Americans' perceptions of university attendance and the implications for freshman year persistence. *Journal of Higher Education, 60*(3), 247–277.

Auerbach, S. (2004). Engaging Latino parents in supporting college pathways: Lessons from a college access program. *Journal of Hispanic Higher Education, 3*(2), 125–145.

Avery, C., Fairbanks, A., and Zeckhauser, R. (2003). *The early admissions game: Joining the elite.* Cambridge, MA: Harvard University Press.

Bahnmaier, K. C. (1988). From the twenties to the nineties: 70+ years of involvement by the Mothers and Dads Association. University of Illinois Archives. Unpublished manuscript.

Baldwin v. Zoradi, 176 Cal. Rptr. 809 (Cal. Ct. App. 1981).

Barnett, M. (2004). A qualitative analysis of family support and interaction among black college students at an Ivy League university. *Journal of Negro Education, 73*(1), 54–68.

Bartle-Haring, S., Brucker, P., and Hock, E. (2002). The impact of parental separation anxiety on identity development in late adolescence and early adulthood. *Journal of Adolescent Research, 17*(5), 439–450.

Beach v. *University of Utah,* 726 P.2d 413 (Utah, 1986).

Becker, J. (1999). *Partnerships with families promote TRIO student achievement.* Washington, DC: National TRIO Clearinghouse, Adjunct ERIC Clearinghouse on Educational Opportunity, Center for the Study of Opportunity in Higher Education.

Berman, W., and Sperling, M. (1990). Parental attachment and emotional distress in the transition to college. *Journal of Youth and Adolescence, 20*(4), 427–440.

Bickel, R. D., and Lake, P. F. (1997). The emergence of new paradigms in student-university relations: From in loco parentis to bystander to facilitator. *Journal of College and University Law, 23*(4), 755–795.

Bickel, R. D., and Lake, P. F. (1999). *The rights and responsibilities of the modern university.* Durham, NC: Carolina Academic Press.

Billson, J. M., and Terry, M. B. (1982). In search of the silken purse: Factors in attrition among first-generation students. *College and University, 58*(1) 57–75.

Bourdieu, P. (1984). *Distinction: A social critique of the judgment of taste* (R. Nice, Trans.). Cambridge, MA: Harvard University Press.

Bourdieu, P., and Passeron, J.-C. (1990). *Reproduction in education, society, and culture* (R. Nice, Trans.). London: Sage Publications.

Bowlby, J. (1969). *Attachment and loss: Vol. 1. Attachment.* New York: Basic Books.

Bowlby, J. (1973). *Attachment and loss: Vol. 2. Separation.* New York: Basic Books.

Bowlby, J. (1988). *A secure base: Parent-child attachment and healthy human development.* New York: Basic Books.

Bradshaw v. *Rawlings,* 612 F.2d 135 (3d Cir. 1979).

Brooks, D. (2000, November 5). What's the matter with kids today? Not a thing. *New York Times.*

Brooks, D. (2001). The organization kid. *Atlantic Monthly.* Accessed October 7, 2002, from http://theatlantic.com/c.atlantic.com/issues/2001/o4/brooks-p1.htm.

Brubacher, J. S., and Rudy, W. (1997). *Higher education in transition: A history of American colleges and universities* (4th ed., Vol. 4). New Brunswick, NJ: Transaction Publishers.

Cabrera, A. F., and La Nasa, S. M. (Eds.). (2000). *Understanding the college choice of disadvantaged students.* San Francisco: Jossey-Bass.

Cabrera, A. F., and La Nasa, S. M. (2001). On the path to college: Three critical tasks facing America's disadvantaged. *Research in Higher Education, 42*(2), 119–149.

Calvin College. (2007). Resources for parents and families of current students. Retrieved October 31, 2007, from http://www.calvin.edu/parents/.

Carey, A. (2004). *Student outcomes: New student services.* Bellingham, WA: Western Washington University.

Carey, A. (2005). *Parent outcomes: Family outreach.* Bellingham, WA: Western Washington University.

Ceja, M. (2006). Understanding the role of parents and siblings as information sources in the college choice process of Chicana students. *Journal of College Student Development, 47*(1), 87–104.

Chickering, A., and Reisser, L. (1993). *Education and identity* (2nd ed.). New York: Jossey-Bass.

Chronicle of Higher Education. (2007–2008). Almanac issue. Retrieved October 20, 2007, from http://chronicle.com/free/almanac/2007/index.htm.

Coburn, K. L. (2006). Organizing a ground crew for today's helicopter parents. *About Campus, 9*–16.

Coburn, K. L., & Tregger, M. L. (1992). *Letting go: A parents' guide to today's college experience.* Bethesda, MD: Adler & Adler.

College Board. (2007a). *Education pays 2007.* Retrieved October 30, 2007, from http://www.collegeboard.com/student/pay/add-it-up/4494.html.

College Board. (2007b). *Trends in college pricing 2007.* Retrieved October 30, 2007, from http://www.collegeboard.com/student/pay/add-it-up/4494.html.

College Board. (2007c). *Trends in student aid 2007.* Retrieved October 30, 2007, from http://www.collegeboard.com/student/pay/add-it-up/4494.html.

College Parents of America. (2007). *Second annual national survey on current college parent experiences.* Retrieved October 30, 2007, from http://www.collegeparents.org/cpa/about-press.html?n=1687.

Crocker, A. C. (1989). Parents funds: Are we asking too much? In L. J. Weiss (Ed.), *Parents programs: How to create lasting ties* (pp. 211–215). Washington, DC: Council for Advancement and Support of Education.

Cutrona, C. E., and others. (1994). Perceived parental social support and academic achievement: An attachment theory perspective. *Journal of Personality and Social Psychology, 66*(2), 369–378.

Daniel, B. V., and Scott, B. R. (2001). *Consumers, adversaries, and partners: Working with the families of undergraduates.* San Francisco: Jossey-Bass.

Detmold, J. H. (1989). Dear mom and dad: Please send money. In L. J. Weiss (Ed.), *Parent programs: How to create lasting ties* (pp. 207–210). Washington, DC: Council for Advancement and Support for Education.

Duffy, J. O. (2007). Invisibility at risk: Low-income students in a middle- and upper-class world. *About Campus 12*(2), 18–25.

Duncan, D. (1989). Organizing a parents weekend from start to finish. In L. J. Weiss (Ed.), *Parents programs: How to create lasting ties* (pp. 53-61). Washington, DC: Council for Advancement and Support of Education.

Erikson, E. (1968). *Identity: Youth and crisis.* New York: W. W. Norton.

Family Educational Rights and Privacy Act, 20 U.S.C. §1232g (1974).

Fass, R. A., Morrill, R. L., and Mount, G.E.J. (1986). In loco parentis revisited? *Change, 18,* 34–41.

Federation of Texas A&M University Mothers' Clubs. (2007). Retrieved October 30, 2007, from http://www.aggiemoms.org/.

Fitzsimmons, W., McGrath, M., and Ducey, C. (2006). *Time out or burn out for the next generation.* Retrieved December 16, 2006, from http://www.admissions.college.harvard.edu/prospective/applying/time_off/timeoff.html.

Flanagan, C., Schulenberg, J., and Fuligni, A. (1993). Residential setting and parent-adolescent relationships during the college years. *Journal of Youth and Adolescence, 22*(2), 171–189.

Furek v. University of Delaware, 594 A.2d 506 (Del. 1991).

Geiger, R. (2004). *Knowledge and money: Research universities and the paradox of the marketplace.* Stanford, CA: Stanford University Press.

Gibbs, A., and Szablewicz, J. (1988). Colleges' new liabilities: An emerging new in loco parentis. *Journal of College Student Development, 29*(2), 100–105.

Gifis, S. H. (1996). *Law dictionary.* Hauppauge, NY: Barron's Educational Series.

Gilligan, C. (1993). *In a different voice.* Cambridge, MA: Harvard University Press.

Gott v. Berea College, 161 S.W. 204 (1913).

Grossi, E. L., and Edwards, T. D. (1997). Student misconduct: Historical trends in legislative and judicial decision-making in American universities. *Journal of College and University Law, 23*(4), 829–852.

Harvard Family Research Project. (2007). Family involvement in middle and high school students' education. Retrieved October 30, 2007, from http://www.gse.harvard.edu/hfrp/projects/fine/resources/research/adolescent.html.

Higher Education Research Institute. (2008). *The American freshman: National norms for fall 2007.* Retrieved February 6, 2008, from http://www.gseis.ucla.edu/heri/PDFs/pubs/briefs/brief-012408-07FreshmanNorms.pdf.

Higher Education for Students from Low Income Families, 1970–2006. (2007). *Postsecondary education opportunity.* Mortenson Seminar on Public Policy Analysis of Opportunity for Postsecondary Education. Retrieved October 19, 2007, from http://www.postsecondary.org.articlesdetail.asp?id=1068.

Hinderlie, H. H., and Kenny, M. (2002). Attachment, social support, and college adjustment among black students at predominantly white universities. *Journal of College Student Development, 43*(3), 327–340.

Hoekema, D. A. (1994). *Campus rules and moral community: In place of in loco parentis.* Lanham, MD: Rowman & Littlefield.

Hofferth, S. L., and Sandberg, J. F. (2001). Changes in American children's time, 1981–1997. In T. J. Owens and S. L. Hofferth (Eds.), *Children at the Millennium.* Oxford: Elsevier.

Holmstrom, L. L., Karp, D., and Gray, P. S. (2002). Why laundry, not Hegel? Social class, transition to college, and pathways to adulthood. *Symbolic Interaction, 25*(4), 437–462.

Hoover-Dempsey, K. V., and Sandler, H. M. (1997). Why do parents become involved in their children's education? *Review of Educational Research, 67*(1), 3–42.

Horowitz, H. L. (1987). *Campus life: Undergraduate cultures from the end of the eighteenth century to the present.* New York: Alfred A. Knopf.

Hossler, D., Schmidt, J., and Vesper, N. (1999). *Going to college: How social, economic, and educational factors influence the decisions students make.* Baltimore: Johns Hopkins University Press.

Howe, N., and Strauss, W. (2000). *Millennials rising: The next great generation.* New York: Harper.

Howe, N., and Strauss, W. (2003). *Millennials go to college: Strategies for a new generation on campus.* Washington, DC: American Association of Collegiate Registrars.

Hulbert, A. (2003). *Raising America: Experts, parents, and a century of advice about children.* New York: Knopf.

Jeanne Clery Disclosure of Campus Security Policy and Campus Crime Statistics Act, 20 U.S.C. §1092(f) (1990).

Josselson, R. (1987). *Finding herself: Pathways to identity development in women.* San Francisco: Jossey-Bass.

Johnstone, D. B. (2005). Financing of higher education: Who should pay? In P. G. Altbach, R. O. Berdahl, and P. J. Gumport (Eds.), *American higher education in the twenty-first century* (pp. 347–369). Baltimore: John Hopkins University Press.

Junco, R., and Mastrodicasa, J. (2007). *Connecting to the net generation.* Washington, DC: National Association of Student Personnel Administrators.

Kantrowitz, B., and Tyre, P. (2006, May 22). The fine art of letting go. *Newsweek.*

Karabel, J. (2005). *The chosen: The hidden history of admission and exclusion at Harvard, Yale and Princeton.* New York: Houghton Mifflin.

Karen, D. (2002). Changes in access to higher education in the United States: 1980–1992. *Sociology of Education, 75*(33), 191–210.

Karp, D., Holmstrom, L. L., and Gray, P. S. (2004). Of roots and wings: Letting go of the college-bound child. *Symbolic Interaction, 27*(3), 357–382.

Keeling, R. (Ed.). (2004). *Learning reconsidered: A campuswide focus on the student experience.* Washington, DC: National Association of Student Personnel Administrators and American College Personnel Association.

Kenny, M. (1987). The extent and function of parental attachment among first-year college students. *Journal of Youth and Adolescence, 16,* 17–27.

Kenny, M., and Donaldson, G. A. (1991). Contributions of parental attachment and family structure to the social and psychological functioning of first-year college students. *Journal of Counseling Psychology, 38*(4), 479–486.

Kenny, M., and Donaldson, G. A. (1992). The relationship of parental attachment and psychological separation to the adjustment of first-year college women. *Journal of College Student Development, 33*(5), 431–438.

Kenny, M., and Rice, K. (1995). Attachment to parents and adjustment in late adolescent college students: Current status applications and future considerations. *Counseling Psychologist, 23*(3), 433–456.

Keppler, K., Mullendore, R., and Carey, A. (Eds.). (2005). *Partnering with the parents of today's college students.* Washington, DC: National Association of Student Personnel Administrators.

Kerr, C. (2001). *The uses of the university* (5th ed.). Cambridge, MA: Harvard University Press.

Ketterson, T. U., and Blustein, D. L. (1997). Attachment relationships and the career exploration process. *Career Development Quarterly, 46,* 167–178.

Lamont, M., and Lareau, A. (1988). Cultural capital: Allusions, gaps and glissandos in recent theoretical developments. *Sociological Theory, 6*(2), 153–168.

Lapsley, D., Rice, K., and Fitzgerald, D. (1990). Adolescent attachment: Identity and adjustment to college. Implications for the continuity to adaptation hypothesis. *Journal of Counseling and Development, 68,* 561–565.

Lareau, A. (1987). Social class differences in family-school relationships: The importance of cultural capital. *Sociology of Education, 60*(2), 73–85.

Lareau, A. (2003). *Unequal childhoods: Class, race, and family life.* Berkeley: University of California Press.

Lewin, T. (2003, January 5). Parents' role is narrowing generation gap on campus. *New York Times.*

London, H. B. (1989). Breaking away: A study of first-generation college students and their families. *American Journal of Education, 97*(2), 144–170.

London, H. B. (1992). Transformations: Cultural challenges faced by first-generation students. In L. S. Zwerling and H. B. London (Eds.), *First-generation students: Confronting the cultural issues* (pp. 5–11). San Francisco: Jossey-Bass.

Lowery, J. W. (2005). Legal issues regarding partnering with parents: Misunderstood federal laws and potential sources for institutional liability. In K. Keppler, R. H. Mullendore, and Carey, A. (Eds.), *Partnering with parents of today's college students* (pp. 43–51). Washington, DC: National Association of Student Personnel Administrators.

Mallinckrodt, B. (1988). Student retention, social support, and dropout intention: Comparison of black and white students. *Journal of College Student Development, 29*(1), 60–64.

Mathews, J. (1998). *Class struggle: What's wrong (and right) with America's best public high schools.* New York: Random House.

Mattanah, J., Brand, B., and Hancock, G. (2004). Parental attachment, separation-individuation, and college student adjustment: A structural equation analysis of mediational effects. *Journal of Counseling Psychology, 51*(2), 213–225.

McDonough, P. (1997). *Choosing colleges: How social class and schools structure opportunity.* Albany: State University of New York Press.

McDonough, P., Korn, J., and Yamasaki, E. (1997). Access, equity, and the privatization of college counseling. *Review of Higher Education, 20*(3), 297–317.

McDonough, P., and others. (2000). *Parent involvement programs in education: Best research and practices.* Los Angeles: University of California, Los Angeles.

Moms and Dads Illinois: Dads Association. (n.d.). Retrieved October 30, 2007, from http://www.uofiparentprograms.uiuc.edu/dads/index.htm.

Moms and Dads Illinois: Moms Association. (n.d.). Retrieved October 30, 2007, from http://www.uofiparentprograms.uiuc.edu/moms/index.htm.

Moms and Dads Illinois: Projects Benefiting Students. (n.d.) Retrieved October 30, 2007, from http://www.uofiparentprograms.uiuc.edu/about/projects.htm.

Mounts, N. (2004). Contributions of parenting and campus climate to freshmen adjustment in a multiethnic sample. *Journal of Adolescent Research, 19*(4), 468–491.

Mullins v. *Pine Manor College,* 389 Mass. 47, 449 N.E.2d 331 (1983).

National Survey of Student Engagement. (2007). *Experiences that matter: Enhancing student learning and success.* Retrieved February 7, 2008, from http://nsse.iub.edu/NSSE%5F2007%5FAnnual%5FReport/docs/withhold/NSSE_2007_Annual_Report.pdf.

N.C. State University. (2007). Webcast series for parents. Retrieved October 30, 2007, from http://www.ncsu.edu/for_parents/Orientation/live_webcast/index.html.

New, M. (1989). Communicating effectively and efficiently with parents. In L. J. Weiss (Ed.), *Parents programs: How to create lasting ties* (pp. 99-108). Washington, DC: Council for Support and Advancement of Education.

Northeastern University Parent Message Board. (2007). Retrieved October 30, 2007, from http://messageboard.chatuniversity.com/neuparent/default.asp?action=10andfid=861.

Oblinger, D. (2003). *Boomers, Gen-Xs, Millennials: Understanding the new students.* Educause Review, *38*(4), 36–40.

Padilla, R., Trevino, J., Gonzalez, K., and Trevino, J. (1997). Developing local models of minority student success in college. *Journal of College Student Development, 38*(2), 125–135.

Pascarella, E. T., Pierson, C. T., Wolniak, G. C., and Terenzini, P. T. (2004). First-generation college students: Additional evidence on college experiences and outcomes. *Journal of Higher Education, 75*(3), 249–236.

Pavela, G. (1992, July 29). Today's college students need both freedom and structure. *Chronicle of Higher Education.* Retrieved March 13, 2008, from http://chronicle.com/che-data/articles.dir/articles-38.dir/issue-47.dir/47b00101.htm.

Perna, L. (2002). Precollege outreach programs: Characteristics of programs serving historically underrepresented groups of students. *Journal of College Student Development, 43*(1), 64–83.

Pew Internet and American Life Project (2002). *The Internet goes to college: How students are living in the future with today's technology.* Retrieved January 29, 2007, from http://www.pewinternet.org/pdfs/PIP_College_Report.pdf.

Rabel v. *Illinois Wesleyan University,* 514 N.E.2d 552 (Ill. App. Ct. 1987).

Rayman, P., and Brett, B. (1995). Women science majors: What makes a difference in persistence after graduation? *Journal of Higher Education, 66*(4), 388–414.

Reisberg, L. (2000, September 29). MIT pays $6 million to settle lawsuit over a student's death. *Chronicle of Higher Education,* A49.

Relyea v. *State of New York,* 59 A.D.2d 364.

Rendon, L. (1992). From the barrio to the academy: Revelations of a Mexican American "scholarship girl." In L. S. Zwerling and H. B. London (Eds.), *First-generation college students: Confronting the cultural issues* (pp. 55–64). San Francisco: Jossey-Bass.

Rendon, L., Garcia, M., and Person, D. (Eds.). (2004). *Transforming the first year of college for students of color* (Vol. 38). Columbia, SC: National Resource Center for the First-Year Experience and Students in Transition.

Rice, K. (1992). Separation-individuation and adjustment to college: A longitudinal study. *Journal of Counseling Psychology, 39*(2), 203–213.

Rice, K., Cunningham, T. J., and Young, M. B. (1997). Attachment to parents, social competence, and emotional well-being: A comparison of black and white late adolescents. *Journal of Counseling Psychology, 44*(1), 89–101.

Riesman, D. (1980). *On higher education: The academic enterprise in an era of rising student consumerism.* San Francisco: Jossey-Bass.

Roarty, A. (2007). Helicopter parents: Do they hover too much? *Student Health 101, 2*(3), 9–11.

Robbins, A. (2006). *The overachievers: The secret life of driven kids.* New York: Hyperion.

Samuolis, J., Layburn, K., and Schiaffino, K. (2001). Identity development and attachment to parents in college students. *Journal of Youth and Adolescence, 30*(3), 373–384.

Sanchez, B., Reyes, O., and Singh, J. (2005). Makin' it in college: The value of significant individuals in the lives of Mexican American adolescents. *Journal of Hispanic Higher Education, 5*(1), 48–67.

Savage, M. (2003). How to recruit parents as retention allies. *Recruitment and Retention in Higher Education, 17*(10), 3–4.

Savage, M. (2006). University of Minnesota parent survey 2006. Unpublished raw data.

Savage, M. (2007). National Parent Program Survey 2007. Unpublished raw data.

Sax, L., Ceja, M., and Teranishi, R. (2001). Technological preparedness among entering freshmen: The role of race, class, and gender. *Journal of Education Computing Research, 24*(4), 363–383.

Schultheiss, D.E.P., and Blustein, D. L. (1994). Role of adolescent-parent relationships in college student development and adjustment. *Journal of Counseling Psychology, 41*(2), 248–255.

Schwartz, J., and Buboltz, W. (2004). The relationship between attachment to parents and psychological separation in college students. *Journal of College Student Development, 45*(5), 566–577.

Severino, G. M. (1989). Orientation programs for parents. In L. J. Weiss (Ed.), *Parents programs: How to create lasting ties* (pp. 69–72). Washington, DC: Council for Advancement and Support of Education.

Shellenbarger, S. (2005, July 29). Colleges ward off overinvolved parents. *Wall Street Journal.*

Shellenbarger, S. (2006, March 16). Helicopter parents now hover at the office. *Wall Street Journal.*

Smith, M. D., and Self, G. (1980). The congruence between mothers' and daughters' sex-role attitudes: A research note. *Journal of Marriage and the Family, 42*(1), 105–109.

Smith, M. J. (2001). Playing the college choice game on an unlevel field. *Journal of College Admission, 171,* 16–21.

Sorokou, C., and Weissbrod. C. (2005). Men and women's attachment and contact patterns with parents during the first year of college. *Journal of Youth and Adolescence, 34*(3), 221–228.

Southern Methodist University. (2007). *Parents news.* Retrieved October 30, 2007, from http://www.smu.edu/audience/parents/.

Stage, F. K., and Hossler, D. (1989). Differences in family influences on college attendance plans for male and female ninth graders. *Research in Higher Education, 30,* 301–314.

Stage, F. K., and Hossler, D. (2000). Where is the student? Linking student behaviors, college choice, and college persistence. In J. M. Braxton (Ed.), *Reworking the student departure puzzle* (pp. 170–195). Nashville, TN: Vanderbilt University Press.

Stearns, P. (2003). *Anxious parents: A history of modern childrearing in America.* New York: New York University Press.

Steinberg, J. (2002). *The gatekeepers: Inside the admission process of a premier college.* New York: Penguin.

Strauss, W., and Howe, N. (1991). *Generations: The history of America's future, 1584 to 2069.* New York: Vintage Books.

Surrey, J. L. (1991). The "self in relation": A theory of women's development. In J. V. Jordon and others (Eds.), *Women's growth in connection: Writings from the Stone Center* (pp. 51–66). New York: Guildford Press.

Syracuse University Parents Office. (2005). *The quest for critical knowledge: A qualitative study of historically underrepresented families at Syracuse University.* Syracuse, NY: Parents Office, Syracuse University.

Taub, D. J. (1997). Autonomy and parental attachment in traditional-aged undergraduate women. *Journal of College Student Development, 38*(6), 645–654.

Terenzini, P. T., and others. (1994). The transition to college: Diverse students, diverse stories. *Research in Higher Education, 35*(1), 57–73.

Terry, R. B., Dukes, C. M., Valdez, L. E., and Wilson, A. (2005). Changing demographics and diversity in higher education. In K. Keppler, R. H. Mullendore, and A. Carey (Eds.), *Partnering with the parents of today's college students* (pp. 11–19). Washington, DC: National Association of Student Personnel Administrators.

Thomas, N. L. (1991). The new in loco parentis. *Change, 23*(5), 32–39.

Tierney, W. G. (2002). Parents and families in precollege preparation: The lack of connection between research and practice. *Educational Policy, 16*(4), 588-606.

Tierney, W. G., Corwin, Z. B., and Colyar, J. (Eds.). (2005). *Preparing for college: Nine elements of effective outreach.* Albany: State University of New York Press.

Tinto, V. (1993). *Leaving college: Rethinking the causes and cures of student attrition* (2nd ed.). Chicago: University of Chicago Press.

Torres, V. (2004). Familial influences on the identity development of Latino first-year students. *Journal of College Student Development, 45*(4), 457–469.

Trice, A. D. (2002). First semester college students' email to parents: Frequency and content related to parenting style. *College Student Journal, 36*(3), 327–335.

U.S. Department of Commerce, National Telecommunications and Information Administration. (2004). *A nation online: Entering the broadband age.* Retrieved October 22, 2007, from http://www.ntia.doc.gov/reports/anol/NationOnlineBroadband04.htm.

U.S. Department of Education, Office of Communications and Outreach. (2007). *Empowering parents school box: Taking a closer look.* Retrieved October 23, 2007, from http://www.ed.gov/parents/academic/involve/schoolbox/booklet2/look.pdf.

Upcraft, M. L. (Ed.). (1984). *Orienting students to college.* San Francisco: Jossey-Bass.

Vivona, J. (2000). Parental attachment styles of late adolescents: Qualities of attachment relationships and consequences for adjustment. *Journal of Counseling Psychology, 47*(3), 316–329.

Waley, P. (2007, August 6). Rider U. officials indicted in student's death by alcohol poisoning. *Chronicle of Higher Education,* p. A30.

Warwick, J., and Mansfield, P. M. (2003). Perceived risk in college selection: Differences in evaluation criteria used by students and parents. *Journal of Marketing in Higher Education, 13*(1-2), 100–125.

Weigel, D. (2004). Welcome to the fun-free university: The return of in loco parentis is killing student freedom. *Reason Online.* Retrieved August 10, 2007, from http://www.reason.com/news/show/29271.html.

Weiss, L. J. (Ed.). (1989). *Parents programs: How to create lasting ties.* Washington, DC: Council for Advancement and Support of Education.

White, W. (2005, December 16). Students, parents, colleges, drawing the lines. *Chronicle of Higher Education,* p. B16.

Wikipedia. (2007). *Helicopter parents.* Retrieved October 12, 2007, from http://en/wikipedia.org/wiki/Helicopter_parent.

Willimon, W. H., and Naylor, T. H. (1995). *The abandoned generation: Rethinking higher education.* Grand Rapids, MI: Eerdmans.

Wintre, M. G., and Yaffe, M. (2000). First-year students' adjustment to university life as a function of relationships with parents. *Journal of Adolescent Research, 15*(1), 9–37.

York-Anderson, D. C., and Bowman, S. L. (1991). Assessing the college knowledge of first-generation and second-generation college students. *Journal of College Student Development, 32*(2), 116–121.

Zirkel, P. A., and Reichner, H. F. (1987). Is "in loco parentis" dead? *Phi Delta Kappan, 68*(6), 466–469.

Zulli, R. A., Frierson, H. T., and Clayton, J. D. (1998). Parents' perception of the value and nature of their children's and their own involvement in an Upward Bound Program. *Journal of Negro Education, 67*(4), 364–372.

Name Index

A

Allen, S., 27, 46, 51
Arnett, J. J., 41, 42, 43
Astin, A., 17, 18, 19, 56
Attinasi, L. C., 60
Auerbach, S., 56, 57
Avery, C., 71

B

Bahnmaier, K. C., 76, 78
Barnett, M., 52, 53, 54
Bartle-Haring, S., 49
Becker, J., 57
Bench, C., 84
Bench, C. O., 77
Berman, W., 30, 31
Bickel, R. D., 13, 36, 40
Billson, J. M., 56, 57
Blackstone, W., 33
Blustein, D. L., 28, 47, 50
Bourdieu, P., 56, 66, 67, 68, 72
Bowlby, J., 25, 26, 27, 28
Bowman, S. L., 56
Brand, B., 24, 27, 28, 31, 46, 51
Brett, B., 50
Brooks, D., 9, 17, 64
Brubacher, J. S., 34, 67
Brucker, P., 49
Buboltz, W., 25, 27, 28, 31

C

Cabrera, A. F., 57, 98
Carey, A., 79, 104

Ceja, M., 14, 58, 63
Chickering, A., 24, 25, 32, 95
Clayton, J. D., 57
Clery, J., 39
Coburn, K. L., 3
Colyar, J., 57
Corwin, Z. B., 57
Crocker, A. C., 77
Cunningham, T. J., 46, 52
Cutrona, C. E., 29, 30

D

Daniel, B. V., 103
Detmold, J. H., 76
Donaldson, G. A., 24, 25, 46
Ducey, C., 64
Duffy, J. O., 61
Dukes, C. M., 54
Duncan, D., 77
Dunster, H., 34

E

Edwards, T. D., 34, 36
Erikson, E., 24

F

Fairbanks, A., 71
Fass, R. A., 13, 39, 40
Fitzgerald, D., 27, 29, 46
Fitzsimmons, W., 64
Flanagan, C., 30
Franklin, B., 67

Person, D., 96
Pierson, C. T., 56

R

Rayman, P., 50
Reichner, H. F., 33, 41
Reisberg, L., 38
Reisser, L., 24, 25, 32, 95
Rendon, L., 62, 96
Reyes, O., 52
Rice, K., 24, 25, 27, 29, 46, 52
Riesman, D., 65, 66
Roarty, A., 7
Robbins, A., 2, 63, 64, 65, 67, 71, 72
Rudy, W., 34, 67

S

Samuolis, J., 29, 31, 48
Sanchez, B., 52
Sandberg, J. F., 16
Sandler, H. M., 23
Savage, M., 7, 22, 77, 78, 79, 81, 82, 83, 85, 86, 88, 89, 90
Sax, L., 14
Schiaffino, K., 29, 31, 48
Schmidt, J., 59, 60
Schulenberg, J., 30
Schultheiss, D.E.P., 28, 47
Schwartz, J., 25, 27, 28, 31
Scott, B. R., 103
Self, G., 50
Severino, G. M., 77
Shellenbarger, S., 3, 8, 13
Singh, J., 52
Smith, M. D., 50
Smith, M. J., 58, 59, 63
Sorokou, C., 26, 47, 51
Sperling, M., 30, 31
Stage, F. K., 59
Stearns, P., 16
Steinberg, J., 66, 69, 70
Stevens, L., 85
Stoltenberg, C. D., 27, 46, 51
Strauss, W., 8, 9, 10, 95, 98
Surrey, J. L., 49
Szablewicz, J., 35, 36, 37

T

Taub, D. J., 25, 32, 48, 49, 51, 95
Teranishi, R., 14
Terenzini, P. T., 32, 56, 60, 61
Terry, M. B., 56, 57
Terry, R. B., 54
Thomas, N. L., 34
Tierney, W. G., 57
Tinto, V., 30, 99
Torres, V., 61
Trevino, J., 54
Trice, A. D., 14, 27
Tyre, P., 3

U

Upcraft, M. L., 78

V

Valdez, L. E., 54
Vesper, N., 59, 60
Vivona, J., 25

W

Waley, P., 38
Warwick, J., 39
Weigel, D., 35
Weiss, L. J., 104
Weissbrod, C., 26, 27, 47, 51
White, W., 37
Willimon, W. H., 40
Wilson, A., 54
Wintre, M. G., 29, 32
Wolniak, G. C., 56

Y

Yaffe, M., 29, 32
Yamasaki, E., 68, 69
York-Anderson, D. C., 56
Young, M. B., 47, 52

Z

Zeckhauser, R., 71
Zirkel, P. A., 33, 41
Zulli, R. A., 57

Subject Index

A

ABC News, 3

Academic success
   as cultural value, 54
   effect of attachment on, 29–30, 52
   parents' concern about, 83
   parents' role in, 23, 31
   as topic of discussion, 8, 14

Adjustment to college, effect of attachment on, 29, 46–48, 52

Administrators Promoting Parent Involvement (APPI), 101

Adults, college students' status as, 40–43

African Americans
   Internet use by, 14, 15
   parental role in college choice by, 58–59
   student-parent relationships of, 52–54
   See also Cultural differences

American College Personnel Association (ACPA), 85

Asian Americans
   emotional support from families of, 48–49
   influence of culture of, 54
   Internet use by, 14–15
   See also Cultural differences

Attachment
   defined, 25
   effect on academic success, 29–30, 52
   effect on adjustment to college, 29, 46–48, 52
   effect on identity development, 29, 48–49

effect on retention, 30, 99
effect on vocational and life choices, 50–51
and gender, 27, 45–46
and race, 52
and residential status, 30–31
See also Parental involvement; Student-parent relationship

Attachment theory
   applied to college student development, 26–27, 31–32, 95
   original conceptualization of, 25–26
   recommended learning about, 95
   separation-individuation theory combined with, 27–28

Autonomy, as developmental stage, 24–25

B

Baby Boomers. *See* Boomers

Baldwin v. Zoradi, 36

Beach v. University of Utah, 36

Berea College, Gott v., 34

Black Hawk parents, 4

Boomers
   communication style of, 94
   as parents, 9, 91, 92

Bradshaw v. Rawlings, 36

Buckley amendment, 34–35

C

Calvin College, 15, 103

Campus Life (Horowitz), 11

Campus Security Act (1990), 39

Cell phone, student-parent communication via, 13
Chicanas. *See* Latinos
Chronicle of Higher Education, 19
Class. *See* Socioeconomic class
College admissions
  cultural capital's role in, 70–71
  independent educational consultants hired to help with, 68–69
  upper-midde-class parents and, 63–64
College Board, 12
College choice
  with higher education viewed as consumer good, 64–68
  parental role in, in low socioeconomic families, 58–60
  and upper-middle-class students, 68–72
College of St. Catherine, 97, 103
College Parents of America, 7, 85, 102
College preparation programs, 57
College student development
  attachment theory applied to, 26–27, 31–32, 95
  new view of, 31–32
  parental role in, 21–22
  separation-individuation theory of, 24–25, 32
  See also Identity development
College students
  as adults vs. children, 40–43
  cultural differences in parental support for, 48–49, 60
  first-generation, parental involvement of, 56–60, 61–62, 96, 98–99
  homesickness of, 31
  residential status of, 30–31
  subcultures of, 11
  upper-middle-class, college choice by, 68–72
  See also Attachment; Communication, student-parent; Student-institution relationship; Student-parent relationship
Colleges. *See* Institutions
Communication, college-parent
  best practices for, 80, 81–82

FERPA restrictions on, 34–35, 38–39
history of, 78
technology used for, 94
Communication, student-parent
  electronic vs. face-to-face, 7
  need- and non-need-based, 26–27, 47, 51
  technology used for, 13–16
  topics discussed in, 7–8, 13–14
Consumer good, higher education as, 64–68
Consumerism, student-institution relationship as, 39–40
Cooperative Institutional Research Program, freshman survey, 17–19
Cost
  of college, 12–13, 92–93
  of parent services, 89–90
Cultural differences
  in Internet use, 14–15
  in parental role in transition to college, 60–63, 96
  in parental support for college students, 48–49, 60
  in parenting styles, 92
  in student-parent relationship, 54–55
  See also African Americans; Asian Americans; Latinos; Native Americans

D

Demographics
  and reasons for parental involvement, 17–19
  recommendations on dealing with, 95–99
Development. *See* College student development; Identity development

E

E-mail
  college-parent communication via, 81–82
  student-parent communication via, 14–15
Education and Identity (Chickering and Reisser), 24–25

recommendations to, on working with parents, 99–100

view of, of students, 42–43

See also Communication, college-parent; Student-institution relationship

Internet

college-parent communication using, 80, 81–82

parent-student communication using, 14–15

The Internet Goes to College (Pew Internet and American Life Project), 14

J

Jeanne Clery Disclosure of Campus Security Policy and Campus Crime Statistics Act, 39

K

K–12 education. *See* Education, K–12

Kamikaze parents, 3

L

Latinos

cultural background of, 54

emotional support from families of, 48–49, 52

Internet use by, 14, 15

parental role in transition to college by, 58, 62, 96

See also Cultural differences

Lawnmower parents, 4

Leaving home

cultural differences in view of, 62–63, 96

parents anxious about child's, 49

Life choices, effect of attachment on, 50–51

M

Media, use of term "helicopter parents" by, 4, 83, 100

Mexican Americans. *See* Latinos

Millennials

diversity of, 98

level of parental involvement of, 8–9

traits of, 8–9, 10, 92

Millennials Go to College (Howe and Strauss), 8

Millennials Rising (Howe and Strauss), 8, 9

Moms and Dads Illinois: Dads Association, 75

Moms and Dads Illinois: Moms Association, 75

Mothers

anxious about child's leaving home, 49

attachment to, 47

impact of, on daughters' attitudes, 51

topics discussed with, 8

See also Parents

Mullins v. Pine Manor College, 36–37

N

National Association of Student Personnel Administration (NASPA), 85

Parent and Family Relations Knowledge Community, 101, 103

National Orientation Directors Association Parent and Family Network, 101–102

National Survey of College and University Parent Programs, 103

National Survey of Student Engagement, 7, 8

National Telecommunications and Information Administration (NTIA), U.S. Department of Commerce, 15

Native Americans

family orientation of, 54

See also Cultural differences

New York State, Relyea v., 37

No Child Left Behind Act, 22–23, 81, 92–93

Nontraditional students, 19, 96

North Carolina State University, 82, 103

Northeastern University

best practices for parent services identified by, 80

Parent Message Board, 82, 102

O

The Organization Kid (Brooks), 17

The Overachievers (Robbins), 64, 71

P

Parent Loan for Undergraduate Students (PLUS), 12
Parent orientation programs, 78, 79
Parent services, 75–90
    best practices in, 79–83
    challenges for, 86, 88–89
    cost of, 89–90
    history of, 75–79
    and parental concerns and involvement, 83–86, 87–88
Parental involvement
    defined, 5, 91
    of first-generation college students, 56–60, 61–62, 96, 98–99
    of helicopter parents, 3–4, 83, 100
    literature on effects of, 8–10
    and No Child Left Behind Act, 22–23, 81, 93
    parents' expectations of, 93
    positive aspects of, 4–5, 22
    survey data on, 7–8
    See also Attachment; Parental role
Parental involvement, level of
    appropriate vs. inappropriate, 85–86, 87–88
    data on, 7, 85
    faculty, staff, and administration concern about, 8
    implications of attachment theory for, 31–32
    of Millennials, 8–9
    student satisfaction with, 7
Parental involvement, reasons for, 10–19
    and cost of college, 12–13
    and demographics, 17–19
    and generation, 10–11
    and parenting styles, 16–17
    and technology use, 13–16
Parental role
    in college student development, 21–22
    in K–12 education, 21, 22–24, 55
Parenting styles
    ethnicity and culture as influencing, 92
    recommendations on dealing with, 94–95

twentieth-century changes in, 16–17
Parents
    college students living with, 30–31
    colleges' need to work with, 90
    concerns of, 83–85
    experiences of, in students' transition to college, 62–63
    FERPA restrictions on sharing information with, 34–35, 38–39
    helicopter, 3–4, 83, 100
    loans taken on by, to finance undergraduate education, 12
    recommendations on working with, 99–100
    responses of, to child's leaving home, 49, 62–63
    return on investment in college education expected by, 13, 67
    upper-middle-class, and college admissions process, 63–64
    See also Communication, college-parent; Communication, student-parent; Fathers; Mothers; Student-parent relationship
Pew Internet and American Life Project, 15
Phone
    college-parent communication via, 82–83
    student-parent communication via, 13, 15
Pine Manor College, Mullins v., 36–37
Postadolescent preadults (PAPAs), 43
Princeton Parents Project, 78

R

Rabel v. Illinois Wesleyan University, 36
Race, and student-parent relationship, 51–55
Rawlings, Bradshaw v., 36
Relyea v. State of New York, 37
Residential status, and attachment, 30–31
Retention
    effect of attachment on, 30, 99
    impact of socialization by parents on, 60

S

A Secure Base (Bowlby), 25
Self in relation theory, 49

About the Authors

Katherine Lynk Wartman is a Ph.D. candidate in higher education at Boston College, where her research interests include college student culture, the first-year experience, college access, and the parent-student relationship. In addition, she is a resident director at Simmons College, where she lives in a residence hall with 130 first-year college women. Formerly, she worked in enrollment management at Colby-Sawyer College in New London, New Hampshire, where she developed and implemented a parent and family relations program. She holds an Ed.M. from the Harvard Graduate School of Education and an A.B. from Bowdoin College.

Marjorie Savage, director of the University of Minnesota Parent Program since 1993, is the liaison between the university and the parents of its 29,000 undergraduates. She has done research on parent programs nationally, and she routinely conducts assessments of her own program to better understand the concerns of parents of college students. Most recently, she partnered with a professor in the university's family social science department to develop two online courses for parents to address issues related to college drinking and college student finance. She is also the author of *You're on Your Own (But I'm Here If You Need Me): Mentoring Your Child During the College Years.*

About the ASHE Higher Education Report Series

Since 1983, the ASHE (formerly ASHE-ERIC) Higher Education Report Series has been providing researchers, scholars, and practitioners with timely and substantive information on the critical issues facing higher education. Each monograph presents a definitive analysis of a higher education problem or issue, based on a thorough synthesis of significant literature and institutional experiences. Topics range from planning to diversity and multiculturalism, to performance indicators, to curricular innovations. The mission of the Series is to link the best of higher education research and practice to inform decision making and policy. The reports connect conventional wisdom with research and are designed to help busy individuals keep up with the higher education literature. Authors are scholars and practitioners in the academic community. Each report includes an executive summary, review of the pertinent literature, descriptions of effective educational practices, and a summary of key issues to keep in mind to improve educational policies and practice.

The Series is one of the most peer reviewed in higher education. A National Advisory Board made up of ASHE members reviews proposals. A National Review Board of ASHE scholars and practitioners reviews completed manuscripts. Six monographs are published each year and they are approximately 120 pages in length. The reports are widely disseminated through Jossey-Bass and John Wiley & Sons, and they are available online to subscribing institutions through Wiley InterScience (http://www.interscience.wiley.com).

Call for Proposals

The ASHE Higher Education Report Series is actively looking for proposals. We encourage you to contact one of the editors, Dr. Kelly Ward (kaward@wsu.edu) or Dr. Lisa Wolf-Wendel (lwolf@ku.edu), with your ideas.

Recent Titles

ASHE HIGHER EDUCATION REPORT
Order Form
SUBSCRIPTIONS AND SINGLE ISSUES

DISCOUNTED BACK ISSUES:

*Use this form to receive **20% off** all back issues of ASHE Higher Education Report. All single issues priced at **$22.40** (normally $28.00)*

TITLE	ISSUE NO.	ISBN
_____	_____	_____
_____	_____	_____
_____	_____	_____

Call 888-378-2537 *or see mailing instructions below. When calling, mention the promotional code, JB7ND, to receive your discount.*

SUBSCRIPTIONS: *(1 year, 6 issues)*

☐ New Order   ☐ Renewal

U.S.	☐ Individual: $165	☐ Institutional: $199
Canada/Mexico	☐ Individual: $165	☐ Institutional: $235
All Others	☐ Individual: $201	☐ Institutional: $310

Call 888-378-2537 *or see mailing and pricing instructions below. Online subscriptions are available at www.interscience.wiley.com.*

Copy or detach page and send to:
John Wiley & Sons, Journals Dept., 5th Floor
989 Market Street, San Francisco, CA 94103-1741

Order Form can also be faxed to: 888-481-2665

Issue/Subscription Amount: $ _____

Shipping Amount: $ _____
(for single issues only—subscription prices include shipping)

Total Amount: $ _____

SHIPPING CHARGES:		
SURFACE	Domestic	Canadian
First Item	$5.00	$6.00
Each Add'l Item	$3.00	$1.50

(No sales tax for U.S. subscriptions. Canadian residents, add GST for subscription orders. Individual rate subscriptions must be paid by personal check or credit card. Individual rate subscriptions may not be resold as library copies.)

☐ Payment enclosed (U.S. check or money order only. All payments must be in U.S. dollars.)

☐ VISA ☐ MC ☐ Amex # _____ Exp. Date _____

Card Holder Name _____ Card Issue # _____

Signature_____ Day Phone _____

☐ Bill Me (U.S. institutional orders only. Purchase order required.)

Purchase order # _____
Federal Tax ID13559302   GST 89102 8052

Name_____

Address _____

Phone _____ E-mail _____

JB7ND

ASHE-ERIC HIGHER EDUCATION REPORT IS NOW AVAILABLE ONLINE AT WILEY INTERSCIENCE

What is Wiley InterScience?

Wiley InterScience is the dynamic online content service from John Wiley & Sons delivering the full text of over 300 leading scientific, technical, medical, and professional journals, plus major reference works, the acclaimed Current Protocols laboratory manuals, and even the full text of select Wiley print books online.

What are some special features of Wiley InterScience?

Wiley Interscience Alerts is a service that delivers table of contents via e-mail for any journal available on Wiley InterScience as soon as a new issue is published online.
Early View is Wiley's exclusive service presenting individual articles online as soon as they are ready, even before the release of the compiled print issue. These articles are complete, peer-reviewed, and citable.
CrossRef is the innovative multi-publisher reference linking system enabling readers to move seamlessly from a reference in a journal article to the cited publication, typically located on a different server and published by a different publisher.

How can I access Wiley InterScience?

Visit http://www.interscience.wiley.com.

Guest Users can browse Wiley InterScience for unrestricted access to journal Tables of Contents and Article Abstracts, or use the powerful search engine.
Registered Users are provided with a *Personal Home Page* to store and manage customized alerts, searches, and links to favorite journals and articles. Additionally, Registered Users can view free Online Sample Issues and preview selected material from major reference works.
Licensed Customers are entitled to access full-text journal articles in PDF, with select journals also offering full-text HTML.

How do I become an Authorized User?

Authorized Users are individuals authorized by a paying Customer to have access to the journals in Wiley InterScience. For example, a University that subscribes to Wiley journals is considered to be the Customer.

Faculty, staff and students authorized by the University to have access to those journals in Wiley InterScience are Authorized Users. Users should contact their Library for information on which Wiley journals they have access to in Wiley InterScience.

ASK YOUR INSTITUTION ABOUT WILEY INTERSCIENCE TODAY!